The Man Who Sold Louisiana

The Man

Who Sold Louisiana

THE CAREER OF FRANCOIS BARBE-MARBOIS

By E. WILSON LYON

NORMAN : UNIVERSITY OF OKLAHOMA PRESS

To My Wife

Carolyn Bartel Lyon

Note to the Second Printing

The Man Who Sold Louisiana is directed both to the scholar and to the general reader. It is a work of scholarship and research designed in style and format to appeal to those who most enjoy learning about the past by reading biography. However, the date of the volume's publication was not an auspicious time, here or abroad, for winning the attention of either the scholar or the general reader. The book appeared in the spring of 1942. For the next four years the demands of World War II and the establishment of peace engrossed the attention of both the American and French people, leaving little inclination or energy for recently published works of history. But despite the circumstances of the period of its publication, the first edition sold out, and for some years the book has been out of print.

The career and achievements of François Barbé-Marbois merit continued recognition, and I am pleased that this biography is being made available again. There is much to be learned from the career of a man whose public life embraced the long period from Louis XV to Louis Philippe in France and from the Continental Congress to Jacksonian democracy in the United States. Over these years Barbé-Marbois was a constant force in Franco-American relations, and as the negotiator of the sale of Louisiana he handled a transaction that determined the future of the American republic.

Except for minor corrections, the text remains as in the original printing. It is a privilege to thank again the institutions and individuals who helped me so generously. I hold in happy memory those in France, no longer living, who assisted me so kindly and pleasantly in the summer of 1937. To my friends, Professor Gottschalk and Professor Rockwood, I express appreciation not only for their services with this book but for their continuing friendship over all the intervening years.

E. WILSON LYON

Claremont, California
January 23, 1974

Preface

*I FIRST discovered Barbé-Marbois during the prepara-
tion of my* Louisiana in French Diplomacy, 1759–1804
(Norman, 1934). *Subsequent research revealed that his
part in the cession of the colony was but one of his claims
to fame and convinced me of the value of writing his biography. This book, the result of my labor and enthusiasm, is
the first full-length study of Barbé-Marbois ever to appear
in any language.*

*The volume owes a great deal to those institutions and
individuals who so generously assisted my research. The
book was made possible by a grant-in-aid from the Social
Science Research Council, which permitted me to spend
the summer of 1937 in France. I am particularly grateful to
those who helped me at the Bibliothèque Nationale, the
Archives du Ministère des Affaires Étrangères, the Archives
Nationales, the Manuscripts Division of the Library of Congress, the Pennsylvania Historical Society, the American
Philosophical Society, the Harvard College Library, and
the New York Public Library. I should like to thank personally Mr. Thomas P. Martin, of the Library of Congress,*

vii

and M. Georges Bourgin, of the Archives Nationales, who provided me with invaluable lists of the relevant materials in their respective depots.

It is a pleasure to record the courtesy and hospitality with which I was received in France. M. André Girodie, Conservateur du Musée de Coopération Franco-Américaine de Blérancourt, made helpful suggestions and provided me with valuable introductions. M. Bernard Fay and Madame Aimé Azam assisted me in Paris. Monsieur M. Baudot, archivist of the department of Eure, greatly facilitated my research during the few days I spent in Évreux. M. Jean Julien Barbé, a distant relative of Barbé-Marbois, gave me free access to all documents he had collected on his kinsman during his own extended service as archivist of the city of Metz. I shall long remember my visit to Rouen and the warm reception given me there by Dr. René Hélot, also a distant relative of Barbé-Marbois, who possesses the latter's manuscript memoirs. Dr. Hélot not only placed this valuable document at my disposal but also took me on a delightful trip through the Norman countryside to Barbé-Marbois' chateau at Noyers.

Some of my friends have been kind enough to assist with the final stages of the volume. Professor Louis Gottschalk, of the University of Chicago, read the entire work and made many very valuable suggestions, especially in matters of style. My former colleague at Colgate University, Doctor Raymond O. Rockwood, read the manuscript and offered much helpful advice.

Chapter VI, "Deportation to Guiana by the Directory," appeared in somewhat different form in La Révolution

Française, *and several paragraphs of Chapter X were taken from my article, "Barbé-Marbois and His* Histoire de la Louisiane, *Correspondence with James Monroe," in the* Franco-American Review.

E. Wilson Lyon

Claremont, California

Contents

Illustrations

Introduction

Most men and women hold moderate views on social
and political questions. They wonder what happens to
people like themselves in such great upheavals as the
French Revolution. Unfortunately, our information is limited because historians generally study leaders of the right
or the left. This book, however, is the biography of a
moderate man who experienced all the changes by which
France passed from the *ancien régime* into the modern
era. It is also a success story which shows the rich opportunities open to the talented bourgeois in the eighteenth
century. A merchant's son becomes a peer of France.

The public career of Barbé-Marbois was one of the
longest in French history. He entered the service of Louis
XV in 1768 and remained in office until his retirement in
1834, four years after the accession of Louis Philippe. At
the outbreak of the French Revolution, Barbé-Marbois
was a successful, middle-aged official who had already
served in Europe and America. After ten years as a diplomat in minor German courts he was appointed secretary
to Luzerne, the second French minister to the United

States, later becoming chargé d'affaires. He adapted himself easily to the democratic ways of Boston and Philadelphia and married a daughter of the president of the Executive Council of Pennsylvania. Shortly thereafter, he was transferred to the service of the ministry of the navy and colonies and named intendant of St. Domingue, then the most valuable of all French colonies. His austere manner and rigid enforcement of the old colonial system aroused the planters, who in 1789 drove him from the island in one of the first violent outbursts of the French Revolution in the West Indies.

The former intendant courageously sailed for France, where he spent nearly a decade trying to orient himself in the new era. He served briefly as minister of Louis XVI to the Holy Roman Empire and as special envoy in Vienna. Like other officials of the *ancien régime,* he suffered from persecution during the Terror. After the fall of Robespierre he became mayor of his native Metz and struggled faithfully to restore order and feed the city's needy population. The department of the Moselle elected him to the new legislature in 1795 and for two years he was a leading member of the upper house, the Council of Ancients. His opposition to the dominant majority in the Directory caused his deportation to Guiana after the *coup d'état* of 18 Fructidor (September 4, 1797). On his return from a two-year exile he found Napoleon Bonaparte had overthrown the Directory and had begun the reorganization of France.

Barbé-Marbois rose rapidly in the councils of the new Caesar. He was soon employed on financial missions in the provinces and in 1801 he was named minister of the public treasury. In 1803, he negotiated one of the most significant territorial transfers in all history, the sale of Louisiana to the United States. Napoleon dismissed him early in 1807 as a result of the financial crisis produced by the speculations of the *Négociants Réunis*. But within a few months the Emperor appointed him first president of the newly created *Cour des Comptes*. Except for the Hundred Days, he remained in this office until his retirement, and earned a permanent place in the administrative history of modern France.

The elderly statesman joined with Talleyrand and his associates in deposing Napoleon and restoring the Bourbons. Barbé-Marbois served nearly a year as minister of justice under Louis XVIII and tried to curb the reaction led by the ultra-royalists. This monarch created him a marquis and accorded him numerous lesser distinctions. Despite an earlier opposition to the Count of Artois, the future Charles X, he enjoyed cordial relations with that prince when he ascended the throne in 1824. Barbé-Marbois' career was unaffected by the Revolution of 1830, which deposed Charles X and placed Louis Philippe on the throne.

For more than half a century Barbé-Marbois was a leading figure in Franco-American relations. As a young man he had known the founding fathers of the new republic, and at one time or another he carried on correspondence with Washington, Jefferson, Madison, Monroe, Jay, and Livingston. The many American visitors who were welcomed to his home in Paris found their host extremely well informed on the history and progress of their country.

Two books from his pen illustrate his profound knowledge of the United States and his interest in that country's past.

Barbé-Marbois was a highly cultured man with an undying intellectual curiosity. Wherever he went, he studied the people and their customs, the countryside and the crops, often recording his observations. His love of letters was deep and abiding, dating from his school days in Metz. As a young diplomat he recognized the value of the new German literature and translated some of Wieland's work into French. One hundred and eight titles in the catalogue of the Bibliothèque Nationale attest the facility of his pen. Most of these are pamphlets, but the books alone constitute an impressive output for one constantly occupied with public affairs.

Idealists will be intolerant of the measures by which Barbé-Marbois managed to remain in office so consistently during such a troubled era. It cannot be denied that adaptability to circumstances was one of his outstanding characteristics. At first he appears a rank opportunist, but this is too simple an interpretation of his character. He did demonstrate considerable political courage in St. Domingue and in his opposition to the Directory. It was only common sense for the returned exile to rally to the cause of Bonaparte in 1800. One cannot condone, however, his excessive devotion to the Bourbons after 1815. Yet Barbé-Marbois should not be classed with such notorious turncoats as Talleyrand and Fouché, for he had taken no part in events that undermined the *ancien régime* and drove the royal family from the throne in 1792.

Considerable thought has been given to the particular

form of Barbé-Marbois' name to be used in this book. His name changed more than was customary even in that revolutionary age, being written in turn as Barbé, Barbé de Marbois, Barbé, Barbé-Marbois, and the Marquis de Marbois. The matter has been solved by employing in the individual chapters the name by which he was known at that moment, retaining "Barbé-Marbois," as he is best remembered, for the title of the entire work.

The Man Who Sold Louisiana

CHAPTER I

A Young French Diplomat in
Saxony and Bavaria

ABOUT the middle of the sixteenth century the French kings turned the expansive energies of their young national monarchy toward the castles of the Rhine. One of the first gains of the new policy was the ancient cathedral city of Metz. The town had been the seat of a bishopric since the fourth century and had long enjoyed great ecclesiastical eminence in Lorraine. Its magnificent location on the Moselle River and its command of the gateway between France and Germany contributed to its commercial importance. As early as the thirteenth century the Holy Roman Emperor had recognized it as a free imperial city. The French made military use of its natural geographic advantages and here erected key fortresses for the defense of the nation. In language and culture Metz became thoroughly French.

The city is built on a hill high above the Moselle, which is here joined by the Seille. Charming old bridges and churches reflect the spirit of the Middle Ages. The main square, dominated by the late Gothic cathedral, has changed very little since the days of the *ancien régime*. In

3

the classic simplicity of its public buildings, one senses again the charm and moderation of the eighteenth century.

Just off the cathedral square lies the Rue Taison, where on February 1, 1745, François Étienne Barbé, a prosperous merchant, and his wife, née Anne Mary, celebrated the birth of François, their first son and the third of their fourteen children.[1] The Barbé family had lived in the environs of Metz for generations. As early as 1532, one Collignon Barbé had tilled the soil at Borny, just outside the city. It is not known which of his descendants made the eventful move from agricultural to urban life, but in 1745 the family gave evidence of a long bourgeois background. Madame Barbé, the daughter of a merchant, was likewise descended from the substantial *bourgeoisie*.[2] Monsieur Barbé took full advantage of the opportunities which eighteenth century France afforded the enterprising members of his class. His business yielded an income more than sufficient for the rearing and education of so large a family, and he was able to provide suitable marriages, business or professional careers for all his children. Such economic success brought political honors from the city and the throne. Louis XV made him director of the royal mint in Metz.

Young François had a happy and carefree boyhood, his parents wisely refraining from overindulgence or excessive severity. Madame Barbé was a typical French mother—practical, economical, firm, and just—and her eldest son was devoted to her. The lad's education was entrusted to the Jesuits, who instilled in him an abiding love of the classics and a profound appreciation of literature. As a small child François showed the deep intellectual curiosity

4

which was so marked throughout his life. At the age of twelve he was a prize pupil and was nominated from his entire school to recite some verses at a banquet given by the city in honor of the Count of Gisors, who brought news of a victory in the Seven Years' War at Hastenbeck over British troops led by the Duke of Cumberland.[3]

The boy was brought up with the expectation that he would enter business in Metz, but an unusual incident led the father to abandon his plan of a merchant's career for his son. A rich woman, known to posterity only as "Madame de F.," lodged in the Barbé home while successfully pursuing a lawsuit at Metz. Rumor has it that she fell in love with the twenty-year-old youth, and that he wrote an unpublished work, *Le Pied de Franchette,* to commemorate their affair. At any rate she was so impressed by François' ability that she persuaded the family to send him to Paris to study law.[4] This was the turning point of his life.

The lad and his servant settled in an apartment on the Place du Palais Royal. Like many a Paris student throughout the ages, he soon found other interests more absorbing than his studies. Young Barbé's vice was literature. At home his practical mother had made light of his writings, even asking how much he paid to have his poems and stories published in the *Mercure de France*. In the congenial atmosphere of Paris he cultivated men of letters rather than his professors and wrote anonymously.[5] He played the violin a great deal until he received a personal call one day from the Duke de Richelieu, whose mistress lived upstairs and did not appreciate the law student's music.

François found it very difficult to obtain a position in

Paris, and his rich protectress decided the trouble lay with his name, a very common one in France. She counseled him, "Take the title of your land, the wooded pond (*Maré du bois*) at Woippy where we went to gather forget-me-nots. Call yourself Barbé de Marbois and you will make your fortune."[6] Whether this be the true explanation or not, by a simple stroke of the pen the youth passed from the *bourgeoisie* to the landed gentry. Fortune now smiled on this adventurous son of Lorraine. Marshal de Castries employed him as the tutor for his children and was so pleased with the young man that in 1768 he secured for him a position in the foreign office. After a brief novitiate in the department at Versailles, Marbois was assigned as secretary to the French legation at Ratisbon, then the seat of the Diet of the Holy Roman Empire. The minister was the Count du Buat, one of the most learned men of his day. The association was invaluable for Marbois, particularly since the two men became devoted friends.[7]

The Empire, then only a weak federation of states, had long ceased to play an important role in European affairs. The Diet therefore had little political significance, and the functions of a minister accredited to it were largely ceremonial and social. The duties of a secretary were likewise extremely light. Marbois, already proficient in the German language, enjoyed the quiet old town to the fullest. He observed the customs of the people and indulged his passion for writing. Disgusted by the flagellations of the Catholic processions in Holy Week, he published an article in the *Journal Encyclopédique,* of Paris, severely criticizing the practice. The Lutheran population rejoiced, but the Cath-

6

olics were furious and the young secretary was fortunate to escape with nothing more serious than a reprimand from the foreign office.

In the spring of 1771 the Count du Buat was transferred to Dresden and again Marbois accompanied him as secretary. The labors of both minister and secretary were more arduous in Saxony, but plenty of leisure remained for literary pursuits. Marbois was one of the first Frenchmen to realize the significance of the new German literature, still largely ignored in France and Great Britain. He translated Wieland's *Diogenes of Sinope* and carried on a long correspondence with the author, soon to become the editor of *Der Deutsche Merkur,* the most influential literary review in Germany. The appearance of some fictitious letters of Madame de Pompadour tempted young François to prove they were false. He wrote replies to the published letters which passed for originals until he showed his friends that the first letter of each line of one of the pages when read vertically spelled his own name. In one of the letters he had the imprudence to criticize severely the French alliance with Austria, and he received another warning from the foreign minister.

In the summer of 1774 the Count du Buat received an extended leave, and Marbois was appointed chargé d'affaires in his absence. His apprenticeship over, he now emerged from obscurity as a diplomat in his own right.[8] The incidents which occupied his attention for the next eighteen months were sometimes of that comic opera character so common to the minor German courts in the eighteenth century. A scandalous article about Louis XVI appeared

7

in a Saxon paper, and Marbois had it suppressed at once, but the chargé d'affaires feared to mention the nature of the accusation and never did so in writing.[9] Vergennes, the foreign minister, requested a copy of the journal in a double envelope, the second marked "for the Minister alone." The article was probably a reference to the well-known sexual impotence of Louis XVI in the early years of his marriage.

One of those strange characters so common in the eighteenth century appeared in Dresden in August, 1774. He pretended to be a colonel in the French army and an illegitimate son of the Prince of Conti. This so-called Colonel Schröpfer claimed to have occult powers and he soon attracted an enthusiastic following, led by the Duke of Courland, an uncle of the Elector of Saxony. Years later Marbois wrote: "I am still uncertain what character to assign to this man. Was he an impostor like Cagliostro, a charlatan desiring a reputation, or was he like Swedenborg mentally unbalanced to the point of believing the marvelous fancies of his imagination?"[10] Marbois at once demanded proof of Schröpfer's identity and commanded him to cease calling himself a French colonel until he could produce his credentials. Schröpfer promised to present his papers, but failed to turn up, much to the embarrassment of his sponsors, who had been very critical of Marbois' conduct. Schröpfer fled to Leipzig where he assembled his followers for a dinner and drinking bout. Later in the evening the party went to a forest; the faker stepped away a few paces and killed himself with a pistol shot.[11]

Soon after his appointment the new chargé d'affaires made the important decision to undergo inoculation for smallpox, the scourge of the age. It was the custom to segregate inoculated persons, and Marbois requested permission to absent himself from the city for nine or ten days.[12] The successful inoculation which he underwent may well have saved his life during the Bavarian epidemic a few years later.

In those days Saxony was a good post for observing affairs in northern and southeastern Europe, where very important changes were occurring. Repercussions of the first partition of Poland in 1772 were still in the air, and Catherine the Great of Russia was just concluding her successful war against the Ottoman Empire. Marbois seized the occasion to collect all the information Vergennes could desire, interesting himself particularly in Poland. With his natural aptitude for languages he undertook to master Polish and for this received the special commendation of the foreign minister.[13] The young chargé d'affaires worked assiduously, determined to please Vergennes and win a career for himself. From his pen came more reports on Poland and information on Russo-Turkish relations and the trade[14] of the British colonies in North America with Saxony. The colonies had opened a new and unexpected outlet for Saxon manufactures.[15]

France had no particular interest in Saxon policy at this time, and Marbois was instructed to avoid a definite stand on all internal questions. It was necessary to be careful in religious matters for the Protestant Saxons were ruled by a Catholic Elector. The finances of the country were in terrible plight, and two bitter factions fought at court. When the Elector made himself commander of the army, Marbois sent Vergennes a report branding him as incompetent.[16] Vergennes, in reply, cautioned the chargé d'affaires to be more reserved in his expressions regarding the Saxon ruler. The foreign minister likewise observed that he found Marbois' description of Sacken, the Saxon foreign minister, obscure and contradictory.[17] The young diplomat received the criticism with such good grace that Vergennes restored him to the highest favor.[18] "It is with pleasure," he wrote, "that I give your zeal the praise it deserves and that I thank you for your exactitude in sending us everything you think should command our attention."[19]

Marbois was greatly disappointed when du Buat decided not to return to his post,[20] for he lost a friend and powerful patron, thus jeopardizing his career. He appealed to Vergennes, offering to remain with the Marquis d'Entraignes, the new minister, if such were desired.[21] D'Entraignes had other plans, but Vergennes assured Marbois a place in the service and a salary of fifteen hundred livres.[22] However, he was occupied months longer in Saxony since D'Entraignes deferred his arrival until January 7, 1776.[23] The chargé d'affaires spent two weeks in acquainting D'Entraignes with the details of the Saxon court and earned the highest praise from the minister, who wrote, "Here he enjoys friendship, respect, and general confidence."[24] On Marbois' departure the Elector presented him with a gold enameled box as an expression of his esteem.[25] There is abundant evidence that Vergennes, too, was highly pleased with his work. The mission at Dresden had been a distinct success.

Vergennes gladly permitted Marbois to accept the invitation of Baron de Breteuil, French Ambassador in Austria, for a visit to Vienna. Kaunitz, the great Austrian statesman, took an interest in the young man, and on one occasion invited him to drive in the company of Casanova, who disgusted Marbois with his fulsome praise of Kaunitz's picture gallery. In Vienna, Marbois first met Barthélemy, with whom he later was to be associated under the Directory.[26]

Marbois visited his family en route to Versailles and received the plaudits of his native city. The Academy of Metz, one of those *sociétés de pensée* so characteristic of the eighteenth century, had elected him to membership on March 9, 1774, but there had been no previous opportunity for his installation. For the occasion, on March 4, 1776, he read some observations on his travels and his life in Saxony.[27] This association meant a great deal to Marbois and for many years he sent copies of all his books to the academy library.

Vergennes received Marbois warmly and soon found a position for him as chargé d'affaires in Bavaria. Folard, the minister there, was retiring after twenty years of service, and Luzerne, the new minister, was not ready to go to Munich.[28] Luzerne, a Norman noble only four years Marbois' senior, was just entering on his first diplomatic appointment. Marbois arrived on July 21 and was presented to the Elector on August 17.[29] Soon after his arrival in Bavaria, Marbois made a trip to the salt mines at Salzburg. In the next few months his reports received warm praise from Vergennes,[30] and it was with regret that the chargé d'affaires on January 18 ended his direct correspondence with the foreign office.[31] He remained in Munich, however, as secretary to the new minister and soon formed a lasting friendship with Luzerne. In the next few months Marbois was often absent from the city. In March, 1777, he went to Ratisbon to look after some matters for his old friend du Buat.[32] His health was bad and he spent some time at Innsbruck, where Luzerne joined him, and they made a tour of northern Italy in October.[33]

At this period European diplomats were much concerned over the future of Bavaria. The famous "Bavarian Succession" question arose from the fact that the Elector, Maximilian Joseph, was without direct legitimate issue, as was also Charles Theodore, Elector of the Palatinate, and heir apparent to Bavaria. The latter had several illegitimate children who were of course ineligible to succeed him. He was very fond of his bastard sons and the Emperor Joseph II hoped to induce him to cede Bavaria to Austria at his death in return for provision for them. When Maximilian Joseph died suddenly of smallpox on December 30, 1777, the Emperor began to put his plans into effect. The bitter rivalry of Austria and Prussia made the fate of Bavaria a matter of general European politics. Frederick the Great hoped to frustrate Joseph II by supporting the Duke of Zweibrucken, heir apparent to Charles Theodore, and he sent a secret agent, Count Goertz, to Munich to present the Prussian plan to the Duke of Zweibrucken.

The unexpected crisis found the French ministry singularly crippled, for Luzerne had also been stricken by smallpox.[34] The full responsibility of the negotiations fell

upon Marbois, who was without instructions from Vergennes. The young diplomat rushed in where cooler heads
would have hesitated and busied himself with the intrigue
of the court. On his arrival at Munich he had imprudently
undertaken a mission in Italy to recover some compromising papers for the Dowager Duchess of Saxony, a sister of
Maximilian Joseph. This scheming woman repaid him
with valuable information during the crisis.[35]

What advice should Marbois give the Duke of Zweibrucken, who now appealed to the French envoy? A wiser
man would have pled lack of instructions, for support of
Prussia's project would violate the principle of the Franco-
Austrian Alliance and irritate the Empress Maria Theresa
and her daughter, Marie Antoinette, since 1774 Queen of
France. Marbois, however, threw caution to the wind and
championed the Prussian policy. Goertz won the Duke to
Frederick's plan, and the following summer the one-time
conqueror of Silesia appeared as a defender of the constitution of the Empire. A bloodless war followed and Joseph
had to be content with a tiny corner of Bavaria.

For a few weeks Marbois escaped unscathed, but, on
April 26, Vergennes wrote that he was reported to have
made improper remarks about Maria Theresa and her son,
the Emperor Joseph II. The Empress had complained about
Marbois to Marie Antoinette. Luzerne was ordered to give
his secretary a severe admonition: "Warn him that if I receive the slightest complaint about him I will be forced to
report it to the King, in which case he may rest assured that
His Majesty will not permit him to continue in the diplomatic service."[36] Marbois protested that he was absolutely

innocent: "I declare to you, after the most careful examination of my conduct, and with a good conscience that I am unjustly accused."[37] Luzerne warmly defended him and ascribed the report to one of the two malicious cliques into which the Bavarian Court was divided. The minister assured Vergennes that he was unable to find "even the appearance of an indiscretion on Marbois' part."[38] However convincing these statements may seem, they were not the truth, as Marbois admitted many years later while writing his memoirs in Guiana.[39] Once again his clever pen had got him into trouble, and he had written an ode which began:

> *Aux Armes, Frederick, la Bavière t'appelle,*
> *Retarde ton déclin par d'illustres combats.*

Such conduct was the height of folly. Despite their denials, both Luzerne and Marbois were now in disfavor at Versailles.

In June, Luzerne thought it advisable to return to France and pay his court to Vergennes. On granting the request the foreign minister warned Luzerne not to leave anyone in Munich to carry on the diplomatic correspondence, a clear distrust of Marbois.[40] Nevertheless, the secretary remained for some weeks, contrary to Vergennes' expectations, and sent several reports to Versailles. Marbois' sycophantic letter on August 8 drew an icy command to leave Munich at once. The secretary left for Paris on September 1, fearing his diplomatic service at an end.[41]

In Paris, Marbois formed a circle of intimate friends with whom he gathered almost nightly at their homes in the Rue des Blancs Manteaux. He has left a charming description of these lovely evenings of music and pleasant conversation. "*Iphigenia* is perhaps being sung, or Mlle de Montry, with trembling hands, is executing a concerto of Becket, leaving out the *andante* and doubling the speed of the *presto* so as to get through with it sooner. This is the hour when, towards evening, I used to come out from my hiding-place and start to tell my pleasant and unpleasant experiences. People listened to me, sometimes with interest, sometimes yawning; people went to the harpsichord, sang, and returned to the corner of the fire; people drew, and chatted about their friends or themselves or the news of the day; people translated Tasso, or spoke, or were silent; and they were always entirely at their ease, as they ought to be with their best friends."[42] For Marbois the most attractive member of the group was Mademoiselle de Montry d'Alleray, with whom he seems to have been in love. His letters to her for the next two years paint a pleasing portrait of their author—an intelligent, witty, romantic, and extremely human young man.

In the course of the next few months, Marbois thought of returning to the legal career for which he had prepared indifferently before going to Ratisbon.[43] While awaiting his fate he tried to shield himself from intrigue by acquiring a permanent position in the bureaucracy. Offices were commonly sold under the *ancien régime* and he purchased the seat of a celebrated retiring councilor in the high court (*parlement*) of Metz, agreeing to pay thirty thousand livres (approximately $6,000)—eighteen thousand livres cash and twelve thousand on credit at 4 per cent interest.[44] The new

Councilor was installed on May 20, the usual waiting period having been shortened in order to permit his departure from France.[45] Marbois was not to return to his native Lorraine after all. A new world and undreamed of experiences lay ahead.

CHAPTER II

In the American Revolution

MARBOIS was now thirty-four. The cultivated society in which he moved appeared secure, and the wit of its salons seemed eternal. Yet the *ancien régime* was already beginning to decay, and a generation of rapid and catastrophic change was about to burst upon the western world. Marbois was destined to participate in more than a half century of political and social revolution.

The prelude to revolution in France came from across the Atlantic. Just before Marbois' arrival in Bavaria, thirteen of Great Britain's American colonies revolted against the mother country and declared their independence. France rejoiced at the discomfiture of Britain and shortly gave secret help to the colonies. Vergennes prudently refrained from public support until he was convinced of the ability and willingness of the revolutionaries to continue the struggle to a successful conclusion. The failure of Burgoyne's campaign and the surrender of his army to the Americans at Saratoga on October 17, 1777, brought France into the war.

In February, 1778, Louis XVI recognized the independence of the Thirteen Colonies and joined them in an alliance against Great Britain. The illness of Gérard, the first minister to the United States, now afforded an opportunity to employ Luzerne as minister and Marbois as first secretary in Philadelphia. The two men accepted with alacrity and on June 17, 1779, sailed from Lorient aboard the frigate *Sensible,*[1] which was accompanied by several other vessels.

The voyage was long and not particularly pleasant. The ship was so heavily loaded that Luzerne had been forced to unload some of the biscuit supply in order to make room for his personal belongings.[2] Marbois was soon sick, and he made a good deal of his illness in his journal.[3] Two severe storms and two calms delayed the fleet and added to the discomfort of the passengers. Some excitement was provided by a brush with corsairs and by the rescue of a sailor who fell overboard from the *Sensible*. Of the 280 men on board, 120 were sick when the vessel sighted land. Marbois wrote of Cape Ann: "The most flowery banks, the loveliest gardens, the most magnificent palaces do not approach the beauty of the rock which I see."[4] He jumped in the first long boat and set foot in Boston on August 3.

The voyage served to give Marbois a foretaste of America and an opportunity to improve his English, for John Adams and his twelve year old son, John Quincy, were aboard. Adams and Marbois liked each other and they spent hours in conversation. "This M. Marbois is one of the best informed and most reflecting men I have known in France,"[5] wrote Adams. He later described the secretary in a letter to the Continental Congress as "a gentleman whose abilities, application, and disposition can not fail to make him useful in the momentous office he sustains."[6] Marbois was a keen judge of people and he was much impressed with the ability of young John Quincy. He urged the father to complete the boy's education in Europe and prophesied for him a brilliant public career.[7] John Quincy helped the Frenchmen with their English, Marbois calling him a better teacher than his father. Marbois, who claims to have known no English at all before his appointment, picked the language up readily and on their arrival in America spoke it much better than Luzerne.[8]

The representatives of Louis XVI were welcomed at Boston with a thirteen gun salute and cries of "Long live the King, the protector of our liberties." "His Excellency and suite landed on General Hancock's wharf about five o'clock the same afternoon [August 3], where they were received by a committee from the hon. council ..., who were waiting with carriages for their reception."[9] They were lodged at the home of Mr. Cushing, who received them "as if he were thoroughly glad to have us staying with him."[10] Marbois found the heavy eating and drinking habits more than he could stand and restricted himself to three meals a day. Like most tourists, he preferred the customs of his own country. The practice of the ladies retiring after dessert and leaving the men to drink displeased him a great deal. He was surprised to find that women wore their hair naturally, without wigs and powder, and did not use rouge on their faces. He was impressed with the simplicity of life, the lack of servants, and the dignity of performing one's own errands and commissions.

The young Frenchman's comments upon Boston and New England life are as interesting to modern Americans as they must have been to his friends in Paris. He wrote on August 14, "This country is charming. Nothing more picturesque could be seen than this harbor broken up by fertile and inhabited islands covered with little buildings which give life and movement to the view. Here and there are rocks which contrast perfectly with the plain and rustic villages." Marbois admired the colonists, who with their simple lives were nearer to the fashionable cult of Rousseau's "natural man" than any people he had ever seen. As he told Mademoiselle de Montry d'Alleray, "These same men who open their doors themselves, who go on foot to judge the people, who buy their own food, are those who have brought about this Revolution, and who, when it is necessary, raise a musket to their shoulders and march on the enemy. And between ourselves, I am not sure that people who have porters, stewards, butlers, and covered carriages with springs, would have offered the same resistance to despotism." Cambridge and Harvard also pleased him: "Cambridge is in the midst of a plain cut in two by a river which bears its name. Several houses, elegant in their simplicity, are scattered about the countryside, and proclaim the comfort of their owners, just as the fine orchards, the crops, and the meadows which surround these dwellings indicate the fertility of the soil. The College consists of five buildings solidly built. ... The chairs are filled by well-educated men, and the plan of study impressed us as well thought out. The revenues of the college are estimated at 60,000 livres tournois ($12,000). The war has considerably diminished the number of students and there are now only 120."[11]

Marbois had ample opportunity to become well acquainted in Boston and vicinity, for the illness of Luzerne's servants, contracted on shipboard, detained the party until September 4. The French were entertained at a reception in the Library of the Museum at Harvard College, the president greeting them with a Latin oration. In his walks about Boston, Marbois was often reminded of "the country around Metz, that splendid country where my friends and family are, and which will always be for me the most beautiful country in the world."

It is fascinating to follow these travelers of 142 years ago. They set out from Boston in a carriage drawn by six horses and guarded by troops three fourths of whom were English or German deserters from the British armies. The second night was spent in Worcester and the following day they journeyed through sparsely settled country to Springfield, where they found the rich farms of the Connecticut Valley. At Springfield the party sent the carriage overland and took a boat to Suffield. The carriage route then ran through Hartford to New Haven. The party visited Yale, which provoked Marbois' criticism by its rule that students who married would be dismissed from the college. As the Frenchmen traveled westward in Connecticut they met devastation wrought two months before by the English. There was firing in the vicinity of Fairfield the day they went through. Luzerne and Marbois passed near New Rochelle, New York, but did not stop to see the descendants of the Huguenots.

General Washington met the minister at Fishkill and
the party embarked with him on the Hudson and sailed
down to his headquarters at West Point, Washington hold-
ing the tiller of the boat. Here they were also greeted by
Gérard, the retiring French minister. From this first meeting until Marbois' own death he regarded Washington as
one of the great men of all time. He eloquently described
their dinner at West Point: "Before my eyes was one of the
most admirable spectacles in the world—the valiant and
generous leader of a brave nation fighting for liberty, I was
moved and my eyes grew moist." Luzerne and Marbois
left camp after two days, Washington escorting them to
New Bethune.[12] The American commander was pleased
with his guests, too, and he wrote Lafayette that he had
"imbibed the most favorable impressions" of them both.[13]
Marbois judged Alexander Hamilton whom he met at West
Point as accurately as he had John Quincy Adams: "If
courage, assiduity, and penetration, mingled with a few
traces of ambition can raise a man above his equals, in a
nascent republic, some day you will hear of him."[14] Generals Knox and Sterling escorted the party across New
York and New Jersey. They saw "the vast college at Princeton, built for the Presbyterians," and went on to Trenton.
They spent the final night of the trip at Bristol and reached
Philadelphia on September 21.

The minister was welcomed by the ringing of bells and
an escort of cavalry, composed of the leading citizens of
the city.[15] Philadelphia was then the largest city in the
United States, but Marbois' estimate of the population at
forty thousand was probably too high. The city pleased

him immensely and he liked its regular street plan. Except for the churches he did not consider the buildings notable for their architecture. He thought the State House, now Independence Hall, "a fine enough mass in the grouping of the city, but it is a tasteless and inelegant structure."[16]

The years of the American Revolution were happy ones for the young secretary. Luzerne acquired a commanding influence over Congress,[17] and he and Marbois were lionized by the society of the capital. The latter's amiability and command of English made him a great favorite, and his popularity was enhanced by his genuine admiration of American institutions. After the first few weeks in Boston his memoirs reflect little criticism of the people of the United States.

Sometime in March, 1780, Luzerne and Marbois received the greatest literary and scientific distinction possible in the New World—election to membership in the American Philosophical Society.[18] The following January, Marbois was chosen a councilor for a term of three years and was reëlected in 1784 for a similar term. He took an active part in the deliberations of the Society, served on several committees, and maintained his connection with it in later life by presenting copies of his books.[19]

In America Marbois showed the deep interest in forestry, horticulture, and agriculture which continued throughout his life. He collected seeds in Pennsylvania and shipped them to France, listing such American trees as magnolia, red cedar, catalpa, all kinds of oaks, persimmon, and chinquapin.[20] He built a botanical garden for his own pleasure and collected 250 varieties of trees and shrubs belonging to North America. One night a goat, a sheep, and several cattle strayed into the city and devastated his garden. His lament was that of a true gardener: "I had a feeling of pain which I cannot express to you. I actually lost my appetite over it."[21]

In April, 1780, the minister and his secretary visited Washington at headquarters—now located at Morristown, New Jersey. They journeyed to Staten Island whence they looked at the British forces through their field glasses. Again Marbois and the commander in chief were charmed with each other. Marbois wrote of "his devotion without limit," and Washington assured him that there was nothing he desired more "than frequent occasions of giving you proofs of the high estimation in which I hold you."[22]

Luzerne and Marbois worked together in perfect harmony throughout their long association in Bavaria and America. Luzerne had complete confidence in the ability and integrity of his secretary, and Marbois was devoted to his superior. Luzerne was often absent from Philadelphia and on these occasions he appointed Marbois chargé d'affaires. He first served in this capacity in the autumn of 1780 when the minister visited Rochambeau and the French army at Hartford, Connecticut.[23] Marbois was ambitious and when in charge of the legation he supplied Vergennes with more than the normal quota of reports. The chief matters of interest at this time were the treason of Benedict Arnold, on which Marbois prepared a memoir which he published years later,[24] and the American controversy with Spain over the navigation of the Mississippi.

On the latter question Marbois, like Vergennes, felt an

obligation to France's ally, Spain, as well as to the United States. In 1780, John Jay was in Madrid endeavoring to make an alliance with Spain, who had already declared war on England in her own behalf. His instructions required that he secure Spanish consent to American navigation of the Mississippi, but Spain refused to become an ally of the United States on this condition. Jay then wrote for further instructions, and Congress considered the matter while Marbois was acting as chargé d'affaires. Marbois joined with Rendon, secretary to the recently deceased Spanish agent, Mirailles, in asking Congress to moderate its stand on the Mississippi question. He advised Congress to solicit the navigation of the river not as a right but as a favor from the Spanish monarch. Marbois spoke privately to representative Jennifer, of Maryland, and they drew up a memoir on the question, urging a reconsideration of Jay's instructions by Congress.[25] That body stood firm in its demand, but Marbois was not without some influence in the affair. He had intimate connections with two or three members of the committee considering the report to be sent Jay, and Madison showed it to him in rough draft. Marbois thought he persuaded him to make it less in the tone of the "ambitious principles adopted by Virginia."[26]

The American cause, at one of its lowest ebbs a few months before, began to brighten. General Greene reconquered South Carolina, and the French at last made plans for effective naval and military assistance. Rochambeau's army was moved from Newport to White Plains, New York, where it joined Washington's forces on July 6. A strong French squadron under Admiral de Grasse sailed up from the West Indies and a smaller French squadron commanded by the Comte de Barras arrived at Newport. De Grasse decided to throw the combined French fleets and the Franco-American army against the strong fortifications which Cornwallis had begun to construct at Yorktown, Virginia, in August. The siege began on September 30, and the French mastery of the sea forced Cornwallis' surrender on October 17. Two years remained before peace would be signed, but the American Revolution was over as a military conflict. Marbois was very active during these crucial months. He served as chargé d'affaires in July while Luzerne was absent with the armies. His reports are filled with news of Greene's operations in South Carolina, the movements of Lafayette's cavalry, and the plans for the union of Washington's and Rochambeau's armies.[27]

Marbois was not too busy, however, to attend the second annual Commencement of the University of Pennsylvania. Six hours of exercises, attended by the notables of the city, were devoted to extolling liberty and Louis XVI. The professors apparently spent most of their time in the classroom denouncing England and George III and trying to create a friendship for France. Marbois reported that the zeal and success with which they fulfilled this duty were beyond imagination.[28]

The winter of 1781–82 was one of the most brilliant social seasons in the history of Philadelphia. Cornwallis' surrender added a gaiety which was increased by the large number of French officers and their families who were in the city. A good many French people also came up from the West Indies. The city had a truly cosmopolitan air, but the prevailing foreign tone was French. "Cooking was French, dancing was French, the French tongue was heard on the sidewalks, in the inns, and at the coffee houses."[29] Marbois was thoroughly at home in both French and American circles.

Earlier in the year Marbois had begun the preparation of a work on the thirteen states individually and as a whole. He submitted twenty-three questions to Chief Justice McKain about the state of Delaware.[30] A similar request to Jefferson on Virginia led to the preparation of a famous book—Jefferson's *Notes on Virginia*. Jefferson had made notes on the state over a period of years and he put them into logical order for Marbois' use. When Jefferson was later minister to France he published a limited edition of two hundred copies, but a French translation and then an English edition gave the book a wide reading public.[31]

Luzerne broadened his secretary's functions on September 28, 1781, by appointing him consul *ad interim* for Philadelphia. The minister wrote Vergennes that Marbois could fill this office without interfering with his other duties, and the foreign minister readily consented to the appointment.[32] In the long run this temporary appointment had an important effect on Marbois' career under the *ancien régime*. It brought him into direct correspondence with the Marquis de Castries, his patron since he first came to Paris from Metz, who was now minister of the navy and colonies. Marbois continued in the consular service until his departure from America, and then he became a full-time employee of that department.

The new consul gave some thought to the development of a permanent French trade with the United States after the conclusion of the war. Fashions, silks, wine, and *eaux-de-vie* were widely sold in the colonies before the Revolution, despite the trade laws, and would need no protection in an independent country. Trade in cloth and hardware, however, required assistance. Knives and forks were badly needed by American merchants, but French styles in these were not acceptable. Marbois suggested that the government bring over several English workmen from Birmingham and let them show French manufacturers how to produce the type of goods demanded in America.[33] While Marbois desired the exportation of manufactures to America, he felt that the government should discourage the efforts of the Illinois, Vandalia, Wabash, and Indiana land companies to attract Frenchmen to the West, since France would suffer by the loss of population.[34]

Luzerne went to Virginia in March, 1782, for several weeks, leaving Marbois as chargé d'affaires as usual. On March 13, Marbois wrote Vergennes a routine letter, opposing the American claim to be admitted to the Newfoundland fisheries by the peace treaty.[35] His letter was merely a reflection of arguments which Luzerne had already presented: France did not promise the fisheries by the Treaty of Alliance, and the Americans would be more dangerous rivals than the English.[36] Marbois, however, made specific proposals to prevent America's sharing the fisheries. He thought Louis XVI might intimate to Congress that the United States could not be allowed to conquer British possessions outside the thirteen colonies. He agreed with Luzerne that France should seize Cape Breton Island, from which she could control the fisheries and suppress smuggling.

The letter would have been forgotten in the files of the foreign office had it not been intercepted by the British, and a copy in translation presented to John Jay, one of the American peace commissioners. Jay, who was already distrustful of the French, forwarded the letter to Congress, who received it on December 23, 1782.[37] Marbois denied its authenticity to Madison, but a copy in the French archives attests its genuineness.[38] Many members of Congress, especially New Englanders, were aroused against Marbois, some even attacking France. The chargé d'affaires allayed the storm by his mendacity, but echoes of the fisheries question followed his subsequent career in the United States. The letter remains, even today, Marbois' best-known activity during his residence in America.

A quiet year followed. British troops remained in America, notably occcupying New York, but the fighting had ceased. Marbois speculated upon the future of French commerce in the new republic, estimating it at 4,300,000 livres for 1782. Most of the trade was in the hands of American merchants, who had difficulty running the still effective British blockade.[39] Philadelphia, for example, received most of its goods overland from the ports on Chesapeake Bay. Marbois thought that a third of the merchandise leaving France for America never reached its destination. On May 20, 1783, he wrote that peace had brought a great drop in prices and that most things were cheaper than in Europe. The only way he saw for French merchants to avoid large losses was to hold their goods and send factors to represent them on this side of the Atlantic.[40]

The end of the war raised the question of trade privileges to be accorded the Americans in France and the West Indies. During hostilities the French colonies had been thrown open to the Yankee merchants, who developed a thriving business in the islands. At the peace, the merchants in France wished to reimpose the former restrictions on colonial trade, and the Americans were therefore very uncertain about the future of their commerce. Marbois took a moderate mercantile position on the matter, but urged that the new government regulations be published at once.[41] His reports at this time present a valuable picture of the attempts of both nations to establish their commercial relations on a peace-time basis. He found that trade in America was taking directions unknown before the Revolution. Philadelphia, for example, had become a center for the shipment of French goods to Havana, despite the vigilance of the Spanish authorities.[42] All the nations of the world had sent their products to America and the market was flooded.[43]

The Americans were angered to learn in August, 1783, that the French government had decreed that American flour could be admitted to the French colonies only in French ships. The exports of tafia and molasses was likewise restricted to French vessels. Marbois favored the exclusion of American vessels, but he thought it advantageous to the colony to permit the continued introduction of American flour, which had been forbidden before the war. He also felt that the trade in sugar between the West

Indies and America was mutually beneficial and should be allowed.[44] Marbois' suggestions were mercantilistic but they considered the needs of the West Indies rather than the interests of the French merchants. The government, however, made concessions to the merchants, and the decree of August 30, 1784, which definitely fixed the relations of the colonies and the United States, put flour and salt pork on the forbidden list of imports. Imports permitted were timber, dyewoods, live stock, raw or tanned hides, furs, grapes, tar, coal, salt, beef, salt fish, rice, maize, and vegetables. Exports permitted were molasses, rum, and goods from France.[45]

A group of American soldiers mutinied in Philadelphia on June 21, 1783, because their pay was in arrears. The uprising was quelled without difficulty, but Congress, in fear and indignation, retired to Princeton. Marbois followed the government in its peregrinations. Early in January, 1784, he was in Annapolis enjoying dinner parties, balls, and cards while awaiting the arrival of sufficient delegates to permit the functioning of Congress. He anticipated the completion of all business—ratification of the treaty with England, treaties with the Indians, regulation of boundaries with Louisiana and Canada, and the admission of new states—within three months.[46]

At Annapolis, Luzerne informed Congress of new arrangements decreed for the French consular service in America. Marbois had been named consul general for the thirteen states. Under him were four consuls and five vice-consuls. Congress cordially approved the new arrangements and the issuance of *exequaturs* was sanctioned on February 11.[47]

Marbois soon effected a comprehensive reorganization of the consular service in the United States. To him belongs the honor of inaugurating the first regular European consular offices in the new nation. This was one of the greatest services he rendered France in his long public career.

CHAPTER III

French Chargé d'Affaires in the United States

THE United States in 1784 was entering upon what historians generally call the "critical period" of her history. It was questionable whether the new nation could preserve its independence in the face of dissension at home and hostility abroad. The thirteen sovereign states were united loosely under the Articles of Confederation, which gave Congress no authority to coerce recalcitrant states or to act on individual citizens. The new government was experiencing the greatest difficulty in securing the settlement of boundary disputes with Great Britain in the northwest and with Spain in the southwest. The impotence of his ally was not displeasing to Vergennes, for he preferred to keep the United States dependent upon France. This was a quiet period in Franco-American relations, and Marbois' chief duties were the stimulation of French commerce and the inauguration of normal peace-time relations between the two countries. His conduct earned the approbation of his superiors at Versailles and the gratitude of the American government.

Of his zeal for the New World there could be no doubt,

for he climaxed a brilliant social career in Philadelphia by marrying one of the most charming young ladies of the city, Elizabeth Moore, daughter of William Moore, recently president of the Executive Council of Pennsylvania. The bride was twenty years younger than the groom. A year had been necessary to arrange the match, as Marbois, careful even in matters of heart, asked Vergennes' permission before becoming engaged.[1] His letter to the foreign minister bared his own personal finances and reflected his plans for the future. He estimated that his income, joined to that of his fiancée (whose name he did not disclose) would allow the couple to live comfortably. Their combined inheritances, plus anything the king might give them, would be invested in land around Metz, where he would eventually serve in the Parlement. Vergennes assented to the wedding and the couple were married on June 17, 1784.

The event was long remembered in the social annals of Philadelphia. The bride, though Protestant, waived all reservations on religion, and a Catholic service was first held in Luzerne's chapel. A Protestant ceremony then followed in the Moore home. Prominent Philadelphians and foreign diplomats appeared as witnesses for the two parties. Marbois was represented by Luzerne, Van Berkel, the Dutch minister, Thomas Mifflin, president of Congress, the French Consul for Maryland and Virginia, and his own younger brother, Pierre-François Barbé, who had entered the consular service in the United States. John Dickinson, president of the Executive Council of Pennsylvania, and Charles Thomson, secretary of Congress, and her parents

34

appeared for the bride. The Moores admitted frankly in the marriage contract that one of the motives for their consent was the elevation of their daughter's social position.[2] Among the congratulations showered upon the young couple none were more cordial than those of Mr. and Mrs. George Washington. Washington wrote to Marbois, "Though you have given many proofs of your predilection and attachment to this country, yet this last may be considered as not only a great and tender one, but as the most pleasing and lasting tie of affection. The accomplishments of the lady, and her connexions, cannot fail to make it so."[3]

Luzerne received an extended leave from America, beginning June, 1784, and he urged the appointment of Marbois as chargé d'affaires during his absence.[4] Vergennes accepted the recommendation, and Marbois served as France's representative in the United States for the next fifteen months. Although at least one member of Congress feared he would play politics with the factions,[5] the majority spoke highly of Marbois' ability and his friendship for the American cause.[6]

Just before Luzerne's departure, Marbois became involved in an affair that caused him untold personal embarrassment and advertised his name all over America. The post-war period was marked by an increase of lawlessness in the country, and the flight of Congress had weakened authority in cosmopolitan Philadelphia. There a number of unruly foreigners were taking advantage of the situation to threaten and intimidate the representatives of their homelands. An attack upon a foreign minister or consul would precipitate the gravest questions for Congress and the state in which the crime occurred. The United States had not yet executed extradition treaties with foreign powers, and it had not faced the responsibility of securing the persons and property of foreign officials resident in its territory. An attack upon Marbois, trivial enough in itself, was to raise these fundamental issues in international relations and international law between France and the young republic.

Among the shady French adventurers in Philadelphia in 1784 was one Charles Julien Longchamps. Though actually the son of a petty merchant at Tours or St. Malo, Longchamps tried to pass as a gentleman, wearing the uniform of the Noailles Dragoons and a medal which Luzerne and Marbois did not recognize. He had been guilty of various misdemeanors in France and soon there were reports of his misconduct in Philadelphia. He appealed unsuccessfully to Marbois and Luzerne for a statement that he was a French subject of good character. Soon Longchamps seduced and married a young Quakeress, to the indignation of that sect. Articles appeared in their papers warning young girls not to go out with foreigners, and the bitter indictments even exceeded the enormity of Longchamps' misdeeds. Angered by these attacks, Longchamps on May 17, 1784, again asked Marbois to testify to his good standing as a French subject. Upon the consul's refusal, Longchamps flew into a rage, threatened to hit Marbois over the head, and stormed out of the office promising to dishonor him at some future time. The threats were overheard by the employees of the ministry and Longchamps repeated his insults under Luzerne's window.[7] Marbois reported the affair to Dickinson, who talked to Longchamps and satisfied himself that the Frenchman would keep the peace.[8]

On May 19, Marbois went to the exchange to make arrangements with the captain of the vessel which was to take Luzerne to France. While returning he was accosted by Longchamps, who began to abuse him in a loud tone. Marbois started to go but Longchamps rushed after him and struck him with a cane, whereupon Marbois returned the blow with a small cane which broke into pieces. They then grappled with each other and a scuffle ensued, until several bystanders succeeded in parting them.[9] Marbois asserted that Longchamps shouted for a pistol and threatened to kill him.[10]

Luzerne and Marbois immediately called on Dickinson, who found himself in a highly embarrassing position. He desired very much to satisfy the French because of his close personal relations with them, but he feared the protest this would elicit from his political opponents. Dickinson several times told Luzerne he wished the minister would seize Longchamps and send him off to France immediately. Luzerne presented a written demand that Longchamps be arrested and returned to France for punishment.[11] Dickinson replied that Longchamps could not be delivered legally under the Pennsylvania Constitution and that his arrest would raise the cry of *lettres de cachet.* The Dutch, Swedish, and Spanish diplomats in Philadelphia were unanimous in their support of Luzerne's request. The flight of Congress from Philadelphia and the general weakness of the government of the United States had placed these ministers at the mercy of their discontented nationals. They hoped very much that an example[12] could be made of Longchamps.

Dickinson decided to have Longchamps arrested and he assured Luzerne that all the resources of Pennsylvania would be used to see that justice was done Marbois. A warrant was issued for Longchamps and he was taken into custody. The president told the minister that the question of the culprit's return to France could be decided only by the judges who were then away on their circuits. "We trust," he wrote, "that either by the desired compliance, or by the infliction of an exemplary punishment, it will be evinced, that the Laws of Nations are properly vindicated in this state." Dickinson was indignant at the outrages "offered in this state to a person so justly and universally esteemed as Mr. de Marbois is among us for his distinguished merit and good conduct."[13] The harassed president also expressed his deep regret to Marbois directly and assured him of his own personal esteem.[14] In the meantime, the chagrined Marbois had sought Longchamps in the hope of defending his honor in a duel, but had not been able to locate him.[15]

The case did not proceed as smoothly as might have been expected, for the accused escaped while the sheriff was returning him to prison, following a hearing to determine whether he should be allowed bail. A reward of $500 previously authorized by Congress was proclaimed at once and circulated throughout the thirteen states.[16] The state of Pennsylvania then offered an additional reward of $500,[17] and within a few days the culprit was returned to custody.

The state authorities were eager to coöperate with Congress in a matter of such international importance and the Supreme Council wrote Congress on May 28 asking its opinion on the case, stating its desire "that our proceedings may correspond with their [Congress'] judgment, and to testify our determined resolution with all our powers to maintain the dignity of the United States, to preserve the public repose, to assert the law of nations, and to manifest our entire regard for the representatives of the sovereignty of the Union."[18] Congress replied on June 4 that the measures taken by Pennsylvania met "the fullest approbation of the Committee of the States."[19]

Luzerne sailed for France on June 20, before the trial occurred, leaving Marbois as chargé d'affaires and therefore embarrassingly entrusted with securing official satisfaction for a personal insult. The minister enjoined his successor to insist on Longchamps' return to France, under guard, or at least his detention in America until the wishes of Louis XVI should be ascertained. If the judges freed Longchamps at any time while Marbois was in Philadelphia the chargé d'affaires was ordered to retire to the residence of Congress, or its committee, and there await instructions from the Court.[20]

The prisoner was tried on June 24–25 and found guilty on two charges: violating Luzerne's house, and attacking Marbois. Judgment was deferred until the convocation of the Council of Judges of the state on July 10. During the trial the attorney general of the state vainly tried to get Marbois to appear as a witness, but the chargé d'affaires contended that it was incompatible with his diplomatic character to recognize the authority of Pennsylvania over him. The attorney general finally dropped the request, saying he had insisted only in order to be "absolutely certain" of making a case against Longchamps but he felt confident that could be done without Marbois' appearance.[21] Illness of one of the judges delayed the sentence until October 8, but then a heavy penalty was imposed. Longchamps was fined one hundred crowns and condemned to remain in prison until July 4, 1786. On release he was to give a bond of £1000, furnished by two men at the rate of £500 each, guaranteeing that he would keep the peace for seven years.[22]

The attitude of the Pennsylvania authorities toward extradition was influenced by the excitement the case aroused. No responsible person raised his voice in support of Longchamps' actions, and there was almost unanimous public consent that he be punished severely. On the other hand the question of returning him to France raised two larger issues which were very dear to the American of that day. In the first place, was America to allow European governments to reclaim their nationals? The extradition of Longchamps might hurt immigration and thus hinder the development of the vast area west of the Appalachians. Secondly, how could the United States claim to be a haven of liberty and an asylum for the oppressed if she surrendered such refugees at the request of their former sovereigns? The question was complicated further by the fact that on the morning he attacked Marbois, Longchamps had taken an oath before a magistrate as an American citizen. His supporters thus argued that France had no further authority over him and raised the cry of tyranny. A pamphlet of June 28 called upon the citizens of Philadelphia to prevent the transportation of the condemned man. "Never have your rights and your privileges known such dangers as at the present. . . . It is the common cause, the cause of liberty, of virtue and of humanity, a cause which should be sustained despite all the tyrants and despots."[23] Sober citizens spoke a milder language, but generally felt that Longchamps should not be surrendered to the French authorities. Although Dickinson told Marbois privately that he thought Longchamps should be returned to France,[24] he very carefully pursued the opposite course in all his public utterances.

The Longchamps affair caused Marbois no end of annoyance and in the long run reduced his popularity in the United States. During the imprisonment and trial Marbois received anonymous letters and was embarrassed by the opposition of the unruly elements in the French colony, who wished to discredit the consular authority. The continued demand for Longchamps' return to France kept the case before the public and the officials as long as Marbois remained in America.

The chargé d'affaires received the warmest support at Versailles, both Vergennes and Castries expressing their personal sympathy. On October 12, the foreign minister confirmed Luzerne's order to request the extradition of Longchamps. If this were not secured, Marbois was instructed to insist on a severe penalty for the condemned and to appeal for restraint upon French subjects then causing trouble for French officials in America.[25] Marbois decided to place his request for Longchamps before Congress, which was then meeting in Annapolis. It is significant that both he and Luzerne first sought satisfaction from the state government, turning to the weak confederacy only as a last resort. Marbois felt, however, that Congress would feel its responsibility in the matter and would readily gratify its ally.[26]

Congress moved to New York and Marbois waited several months before requesting the surrender of Longchamps. In the meantime, Marbois' indignation over his own personal affront had given way to sympathy for the unfortunate man, whom he felt to have been punished too severely. He had expressed this sentiment on January 6, 1785, and urged that Louis XVI pardon Longchamps at once if he were returned to France. If Congress failed to give him up, Marbois announced that he was going to solicit his pardon in Philadelphia.[27] Marbois' wife also interceded for Longchamps. Perhaps the most interesting feature of this extraordinary case was the appeal of Madame Marbois to Marie Antoinette, as one woman to another, asking that she intercede to secure clemency for her husband's assailant.[28] The Marbois family was either very generous or much alarmed by the turn the case had taken.

On February 10, Marbois formally asked John Jay, Secretary for Foreign Affairs, for the extradition of Longchamps, at the same time revealing confidentially Madame Marbois' efforts in the man's behalf. The chargé d'affaires appealed to Jay to check the "licentiousness of the press," which he felt was aimed at producing strained relations between the two countries. The same day Marbois received a friendly anonymous letter from Philadelphia warning him that it would not be safe for him to return from New York to that city.[29] Jay reported the facts of the case to Congress and concluded that foreigners guilty of crime should be punished by the state in which the crime had been committed. Since this had been done in the case of Longchamps, "your Secretary is therefore of opinion that the requisition in question is premature."[30] Congress delayed any definite action until it could consider the matter "in all those lights which their responsible situation and limited powers renders indispensable."[31] They wished to support Pennsylvania, which had public opinion behind it, and at the same time not ruffle France. Contrary to the usual rule, this attempt to please both parties succeeded admirably. Vergennes wrote Marbois that France was ready to accept the decision of the Pennsylvania court rather than raise further questions.[32] Meanwhile Congress on April 27, 1785, had adopted a resolution asking the states to pass special laws for the protection of representatives of foreign powers. In September, 1785, just before his departure from America, Marbois withdrew his government's request and asked for a return of all papers concerning the case.[33]

So ended *l'affaire Longchamps,* which for more than a year had aroused comment and controversy in America. That it weakened Marbois' popularity seems clear. The case raised fundamental questions regarding the safety of foreign officials in the United States and the power of Congress to protect them. It was a valuable lesson to the new nation in the responsibilities of a sovereign power, and the government took measures to secure in the future the persons and property of the diplomats accredited to it.[34]

43

In the autumn of 1784, Marbois' insatiable curiosity and his zeal for the consular service carried him on an eventful journey to the land of the Oneida Indians in central New York, an area just being settled by the white man. Congress was sending commissioners to negotiate a treaty with the Iroquois, and Marbois decided to accompany them. The presence of Lafayette, who had just returned from France, gave unusual significance to the trip. Some of his American friends persuaded the easily flattered general that he had great influence with the Indians and that he should assist the American negotiators in securing the treaty.

It is difficult for the modern traveler in a crack New York Central train to imagine the conditions met by the Franco-American party in the Hudson and Mohawk valleys. From New York, Marbois took a sloop which transported him to Albany in three days. There he met Lafayette and James Madison, then a delegate from Congress, and joined their party, acting as cook for the group. The roads were so bad that they gave up their carriages at German Flats and proceeded on horseback. At Fort Schuyler they found Samuel Kirkland, the famous missionary to the Indians, and shared his cabin. The party arrived at the fort on September 29 and the following day went to Oneida Castle, some eighteen miles away. There Marbois found Grasshopper, an old chief who had visited Philadelphia in 1781, still wearing a Bavarian hunting costume Luzerne had presented him on that occasion. On their return to the fort the party found representatives of the Indian tribes assembled, and the Oneidas were publicly reconciled to the Senecas. Marbois said it all reminded him of the Diet

44

at Ratisbon! The Frenchmen did not await the negotiation of the treaty but rented a boat and went down the Mohawk River to Albany "in the finest weather in the world."[35] The chargé d'affaires was much impressed by the ravages of the bitter war in the fertile valley and he foresaw great hardships for the Loyalists who were already returning, under the supposition that they were protected by the peace treaty.

The most interesting result of Marbois' trip was a plan for withdrawing the fur trade from British control and conducting it across New York State under French direction.[36] He quickly perceived the possibility of utilizing the natural transportation facilities which later built the prosperity of the Empire State. The furs could be brought from the Great Lakes region, through Oneida Lake into the Mohawk River, with a portage at Little Falls, then to Schenectady, where another portage was necessary, and then to Albany and down the Hudson to New York. He felt such a route would steal the business away from the British even if they kept Oswego, Detroit, and Michilimackinac, which they were not evacuating, as the treaty provided. Marbois' proposal was far sighted and would have strengthened the role of French commerce in America, but, like so many other pertinent suggestions during the *ancien régime,* it never emerged from the pigeonholes of Versailles.

Marbois' last year in America was passed in attendance on Congress, and in the collection of information regarding the extension of trade with France's ally. After his return from the Mohawk Valley he journeyed to Trenton where Congress was sitting. He found so few delegates on hand that the opening session was not expected to take place before a fortnight. Here he met Colonel James Monroe, who had just returned from Montreal bringing a very pessimistic report on the possibility of good relations with Canada.[37] Marbois also busied himself in an attempt to settle the dispute between the United States and Spain relative to the limits of Louisiana and the Floridas. He wrote Congress that Louis XVI would be pleased at any measures taken to promote an understanding between the two countries.[38]

Marbois' dispatches at this time afford a picture of a government without power and almost without organization. On November 20, Congress had not yet begun its session. "There is no Congress, no committee, no President, no minister of any department. All affairs, especially the finances, are falling into a confusion even worse than in the past."[39] Eventually a quorum assembled and after several weeks in Trenton, Congress moved to New York, which remained the capital until the return to Philadelphia in 1791. Some of the delegates told Marbois that Philadelphia was rejected because Congress felt that Louis XVI would not allow the French minister to live in the state which had refused to surrender Longchamps.[40]

Just before leaving Trenton, Congress appointed John Jay as Secretary for Foreign Affairs. This able man put order into his department and gave prompt attention to Marbois' communications. The first of these concerned the portraits of Louis XVI and Marie Antoinette which had just arrived as a present for the American government. A committee of Congress decided to bring the portraits to New York and hang them in the hall where the sessions were held. Jay asked Robert Morris, the well-known financier, to get the pictures from Marbois and store them in his own home until the season would permit their safe transportation to New York. As relations between Morris and Marbois were already strained, the stage was set for the angry exchange which now occurred. When Morris sent his agents for the portraits, Marbois refused to deliver them on the ground that it was not fitting to hang them in Morris' drawing room and that their installation in a private home would necessitate an extra removal and unscrewing of the eight piece frames. (The pictures were eight by fourteen feet). When Morris' servants returned a second time, Marbois refused again, asserting that it was impossible to place the framed portraits in the upstairs of any house in Philadelphia. He announced to Morris that the season was good and he planned himself to transport the portraits to New York. Morris replied in hot anger, denying that he ever intended to display the portraits in his home. "It was not my contemplation to screw and unscrew, to put them up and take them down, or make any ostentatious show of them. The veneration which I entertain for their Majesties, the respect I bear to Congress, and trust reposed by Mr. Jay forbid such an idle display of vanity, as you have done me the honor to suppose was intended on my part." Marbois tried to soothe his feelings by saying the misunderstanding was due entirely to the erroneous assertions of Morris' servants. Jay apologized to Morris for drawing him into such an unpleasant affair and assured him that his conduct

47

had been "perfectly proper."[41] The portraits were delivered in New York but in some unknown manner they have completely disappeared.[42] Were they simply lost in the moving of the government to Washington, or did some ardent American *sans culotte* think them unfit to decorate the halls of a free people and thus destroy them after the outbreak of the French Revolution?

Marbois was preoccupied with family and domestic affairs at this time. His presence in Philadelphia was due to the expected arrival of his first child.[43] The baby, a girl, was born on April 2, and was christened Marie Anne Sophie. Following his marriage, Marbois had occupied the house Luzerne had rented in Philadelphia. In leaving it the chargé d'affaires experienced the usual trials with landlords, and the common problem of disposing of some of his possessions. Luzerne had added five rooms in the attic, a dining room, a staircase, and several closets, while Marbois had constructed a stable, a haymow, and a coach house. They naturally hoped for compensation, but the landlord showed little interest. Marbois presented an itemized statement of the cost of these improvements, but the extant records do not indicate whether he received satisfaction from the owner of the house. The lease expired on April 20 and Marbois was off forthwith to New York.[44]

Marbois decided to follow Congress and take up his abode permanently in New York. He called the French merchants of Philadelphia together and took leave of them in a moving ceremony. His brother remained behind in the capacity of vice-consul. Marbois found his duties in New York no less arduous than they had been in Philadelphia.

On his arrival he organized the French merchants in New York into an assembly. This was the first concerted attempt to sponsor French commerce in the city, which had only recently been evacuated by the British.[45] Marbois' reports from the new capital discussed the misfortunes of the Loyalists, the difficulties of collecting debts due Europeans by Americans, relations with the Indians, the opening and sale of western lands, and the phenomenal growth of "Kentucke." These letters reveal an unusual grasp of American affairs. Marbois continued his travels as time permitted and spent a good deal of the spring and summer touring Long Island.[46]

His days in the United States, however, were drawing to a close. At Castries' request, and with Vergennes' consent, Louis XVI on June 5 appointed him intendant of St. Domingue.[47] On leaving the diplomatic career, he received warm commendation from Vergennes for "his zeal, his ability, and his prudence."[48] There is no documentary proof that Marbois requested the change. He says in his memoirs that since the undersecretaries in the foreign office were hostile to him and blocked his further advance Castries suggested the intendancy of St. Domingue,[49] where his talents would be invaluable and where he could continue in the department of an old friend. Probably a more fundamental reason for Marbois' leaving the foreign service was a social one. He did not belong to the circle of great nobles from whom the ambassadors of the *ancien régime* were drawn. It was simply not a part of the system that a member of the *bourgeoisie* of Metz should represent His Most Christian Majesty in one of the great courts of the eighteenth century. Marbois' rapid rise in the service led only to disappointment—the view from Mount Nebo, but the realization that he could not cross over into the Promised Land. He was not at all downcast over the appointment to St. Domingue. Since a ministry was beyond his reach, Marbois wes pleased to accept the new post. The intendancy of this important possession was universally regarded as more desirable than the position of secretary, consul general, or chargé d'affaires in the United States. The isle was not so distant from America but that he could maintain his friendships in the United States and Madame Marbois could visit her family.[50]

Marbois' successor was none other than Otto, who years before had served as his secretary in Munich and had been for a time in America with Luzerne. Otto's arrival on August 25 marked a happy reunion of old friends. The new chargé d'affaires found Marbois celebrating the birthday of Louis XVI at his home on Long Island. Among the many guests for the occasion were a number of members of Congress.[51] "The announcement of M. de Marbois' promotion in which everyone took the greatest interest added to the gaiety and the pleasure of the company." Otto brought Marbois the first knowledge of his new appointment.[52] The French government had dispatched Otto to America at once, since Castries was anxious to have Marbois in St. Domingue as soon as possible.

Marbois' departure was the occasion for a slight display of opposition to him. An anonymous letter of August 20 to Vergennes had asked for his removal on the ground that he was "entirely disliked by every citizen amongst us, and we truly confess we believe he never will be otherways as long as he lives."[53] When Congress considered the manner of expressing its appreciation of his conduct, a delegate from Massachusetts, remembering the intercepted fisheries dispatch, objected to the phrase "entire satisfaction." After some debate, Congress compromised by deciding on "great satisfaction."[54]

Such opposition was overwhelmed by the general praise of Marbois' work and his conduct in America. Otto wrote: "It is impossible for an officer of His Majesty in a foreign country to be more generally esteemed than my predecessor has been in America. In addition to his work as chargé d'affaires and as Secretary of the Legation, he has placed the different consulates of the country on the best possible footing. If these consulates have acquired some stability, their success is due in large measure to the indefatigable zeal of M. de Marbois."[55] Washington wrote: "I shall remember with pleasure, Sire, the friendship you have always expressed for me, and with gratitude shall recollect the many instances of your partiality and attention towards me."[56] Jay added a personal touch to his official farewell communication: "We have been laborers in the same great work, and I flatter myself that your removal from America will not diminish your affection for it. It will always give me pleasure to hear of your health and happiness, and that of your amiable lady."[57]

Marbois' reply to Jay revealed a deep attachment to the new republic: "I have obtained the principal object of my mission, which has been to promote as much as is in my power, the good understanding and preserve the friendship between the King and the States. . . . Six years' residence, which I shall ever consider as the most interesting of my life past, both by the importance and the success of the events to which I have been an active witness, and the connexion I have formed, will never permit me to be a stranger to America, and I shall be happy whenever duty will concur with my inclination, to afford me the means of evincing the sentiment I shall preserve for it."[58]

Little did Marbois realize when he sailed with his wife and young daughter, on September 25, that he was seeing American soil for the last time. Although Madame Marbois returned for at least one visit to her family, her husband was not so privileged. Yet America left an abiding impression upon him, and he cherished the deepest affection for the new nation. It must not be thought, however, that residence in the United States transformed Marbois into an ardent advocate of reform at home. He lacked the fervor, and dissatisfaction with the *ancien régime,* that caused Lafayette to draw inspiration from his American experience for challenging the established order in France. At his departure from this country, Marbois was an eminently successful civil servant, sympathetic toward liberal ideas, but on the whole well satisfied with the world as he found it. Louis XVI could not have asked for a more loyal subject.

CHAPTER IV

Last Intendant of the Ancien Régime in St. Domingue

ST. Domingue, today the Republic of Haiti, was the fairest French colony of the *ancien régime*. Its exports of sugar and coffee created a rich planter class which lived in ease on the island and exercised tremendous influence at Versailles. Beneath the fifty thousand whites were fifty thousand free mulattoes, and five hundred thousand negro slaves, still completely submissive to their masters.

The government of the colony was entrusted to a governor, an intendant, and a superior council, in which these two officials had seats. The governor was in charge of the general administration and the military forces, which in peace time numbered around three thousand. The intendant, as in France, was primarily concerned with finance, collection of taxes, provision for the armed forces, and the upkeep of the royal property. A number of functions were administered jointly by the governor and the intendant: religious affairs, inspection of courts, agriculture, commerce, shipping, permission to free slaves, hunting, fishing, care of rivers, handling of flood water, policing of harbors, building and care of roads, *corvées,* and the nomination of various judicial officials. The method of breaking a dead-lock between the heads of the government was extremely unsatisfactory, and absolute harmony between governor and intendant was essential for the prosperity and safety of the island.[1]

Marbois and his family arrived at Le Cap, in the northern part of the colony, on October 22 after a poor voyage.[2] He received a splendid welcome, due to Castries' recommendations, but he saw at once that he had stepped into a very trying situation. Everyone he met warned him against someone else at Port-au-Prince, the capital, to which he proceeded by boat eight or ten days later.

Affairs of St. Domingue were indeed in a bad state in 1785, and a difficult task confronted the new governor and the new intendant. Fortunately for Marbois, he was to enjoy the most cordial relations with his superior during the first three and one-half years of his administration. The first governor with whom he worked was the Count of Luzerne, brother of the former minister to America. The preceding regime had amassed a debt of approximately $1,400,000, had failed to file the proper financial statements, and had allowed corruption to thrive. Castries wrote: "One can not deny that a general spirit of graft reigns in St. Domingue." Marbois received stern orders to stamp it out,[3] and for a man of his disposition one such instruction was enough.

The colony had three administrative divisions, the north with Le Cap as the chief city, the west containing Port-au-Prince, and the south, with Les Cayes as the principal town. Superior Councils sat at Le Cap and Port-au-

Prince, but there was none at Les Cayes. A royal act of February, 1786, uniting the two superior councils[4] was destined to make serious trouble for Marbois, partisan of the new arrangement. The suppression of the Council at Le Cap and the concentration of all important administrative and judicial business at Port-au-Prince was no doubt efficient, but it aroused deep resentment in the north. The suppression of the Council was one of the factors that led to bitter hatred of Marbois by an important faction at Le Cap.

The south was by far the poorest part of the island and it complained constantly of neglect. Marbois decided to investigate the situation there for himself. He encountered evidence of smuggling on every hand, most of the commerce being in the hands of foreigners. But the officers were so linked up with the smugglers that convictions were impossible. He was impressed with the richness of the soil, which he had thought poor, and he urged that French commerce try to provide for the area. He recommended extensive public works at Les Cayes, and the stationing of a large body of troops in its environs.[5]

Throughout the colony the intendant encountered the all too common philosophy that cheating the government is not dishonesty. Colonials generally journeyed to France on government vessels without paying a sou,[6] or secured free admission to the government hospitals.[7] A serious fraud in the government warehouse at Le Cap led Marbois to go there personally and dismiss the compromised officials.[8] Most of the merchants of the city had conspired with the government employees in the fraud. His vigorous action, which Marbois calculated saved $30,000,[9] served as such an object lesson that he had no serious trouble with grafters during the remainder of his administration. There followed a long period of routine work. The intendant's reports are concerned with a great drouth in 1786,[10] physical changes in the offices,[11] the introduction of negroes in the south,[12] all sorts of problems relating to slaves, proposals for a hospital for venereal diseases, and relations with Santo Domingo. He secured preferment from the minister for two of his brothers at this time, one in St. Domingue, the other in Mauritius.[13]

During the years of Marbois' intendancy the French government made extensive efforts to introduce new plants into St. Domingue. Such work was very congenial to Marbois and Luzerne, who were both much interested in agricultural experimentation. They proposed the introduction of the cinchona tree and the production of quinine, and they were enthusiastic over the prospect of bringing bread-fruit trees from the East Indies. The famous voyage of the British ship, *The Bounty,* is but one example of attempts made to acclimatize this tree in the West Indies. Marbois and Luzerne felt there were many plants in Mauritius, Isle de Bourbon, Senegal, and Guiana which had never been tried in St. Domingue and which should thrive there. They requested that a young botanist, M. Richard, then in Guiana, be allowed to come to St. Domingue to direct the experimentation.[14] Such interest arose in the colony that the Chamber of Commerce at Port-au-Prince proposed the establishment of a botanical garden, but the governor and intendant thought the existing royal garden there sufficient. A slight extension would enable it to serve the colony quite adequately. The garden was close to the sea and plants could be shipped by water to all parts of the island.[15] In the next three years several cargoes of seeds and plants were obtained from various parts of the world. On February 4, 1788, a sloop, the *Sincère,* returned from Guiana with a number of plants, most of them in good condition.[16] That autumn twenty-five palm seeds were distributed for cultivation by individuals, and 150 seeds of a tree called in Mauritius *arbre à graisse* were planted.[17] A private vessel, the *Alexander,* brought eighty-seven different species of plants at the end of 1788. Among them were clove, breadfruit, camphor, and pear trees.[18] The following year the *Stanislas* brought from India a great collection including camellias, mangoes, and fifty stalks of a new variety of sugar cane, said to yield one-sixth more sugar than that grown in St. Domingue.[19]

Foreign commerce presented perennial problems for the intendant. While a strict mercantilistic policy was followed in general, certain exceptions were made, and these were the loophole for serious abuses. The Spaniards, as France's allies, were exempted from all the prohibitory laws, even the payment of import and export duties.[20] Commerce in certain commodities was permitted with the United States, but the full war-time privileges enjoyed by their ships during the American Revolution made it difficult to keep them in legal channels. Relations with American merchants were further complicated by the fact that during times of distress it was occasionally necessary to remove some of the normal commercial restrictions. Toward the end of 1786, Luzerne and Marbois asked the minister whether foreign flour might be introduced, because of the high price then prevailing in St. Domingue. Castries replied that flour was the commodity from which French merchants drew their chief profit in the colony, and that the trade should not be opened to foreigners except in the greatest emergency.[21]

The minister of the navy and colonies was well pleased with the work of his friend and protégé in the colony. He praised him liberally for the order emerging in the finances and for his splendid coöperation with Luzerne.[22] A few days after commending Marbois' firmness and knowledge of the duties of his office, Castries was replaced at the ministry by the Count of Luzerne. Marbois and Luzerne were exchanging sharp remarks in the Superior Council over the trial of a smuggler when a cannon shot announced the arrival of a boat from France. A personal letter was brought in to Marbois from Castries saying: "Your friend is no longer your minister, but the person the king has appointed is no less your friend than I am." Luzerne read his own letter of appointment, turned and embraced Marbois. Their passing anger was forgotten in the general gaiety.[23] The appointment was not known in France until Luzerne's arrival, when it was announced by a circular on December 23, 1787. Montmorin had served as minister in the interim. Vincent became commander in St. Domingue until the arrival of Marquis du Chilleau, the new governor.

Marbois' regime was marked by great progress in public works. Repairs were made on the theater in Port-au-

Prince.[24] A road was built to Jacmel on the southern coast, and another begun to Le Cap.[25] The suppression of the Superior Council in the north made improved communication more necessary than ever. Toward the end of 1787 fear of war with England led Vincent and Marbois to put the island in a state of defense.[26]

His uncompromising administration bore fruit and Marbois was able to publish a flattering statement of the colony's finances. All accounts were paid when presented, and since April 1, 1786, the government had never paid over the market price for commodities, often receiving them for 5 or 10 per cent less.[27] However, such a record made enemies among those who formerly dipped in the public treasury, and an attack on the administration was published in several papers in Europe. The government put articles supporting Marbois in *La Gazette de Leyde* and the *Courrier de l'Europe,* and Luzerne wrote Marbois telling him to be reassured completely on the outcome of the affair.[28]

Chilleau's arrival in December, 1788, marked the end of Marbois' happy coöperation with the governor. The enforcement of the mercantile legislation brought the intendant into inevitable conflict with the leading colonials, who wished to buy and sell in the markets of the world. In the general ferment which now began to sweep over France, the discontented group became more outspoken. Marbois' critics had won the new governor to their point of view, and he arrived in St. Domingue convinced that the existing regime was far too strict. The intendant's bitter enemies in the colony seized the opportunity to split the administration and soon succeeded in producing a state of open hostility between the two men. Trouble began at least as early as March 19, 1789, when the governor ordered the occupation of certain government houses at Le Cap and Fort Dauphin without consulting Marbois. As the guardianship of public property was a common function of the two officials, Marbois was correct in protesting, but the tone of his objections indicates that relations were already strained. He requested an interview "for treating the points on which we might have different opinions" and prepared a written list under the title, "points to treat with the General, conference of March 20."[29]

Amid the increasing difficulties, the ten-year exile's thoughts turned again to his native Metz. The desire to introduce his wife and two children to his family led him to request permission to return to France the following year. It would be necessary to defer the departure from St. Domingue for several months as Elizabeth Laura, the youngest child, was then only eight months old,[30] and the health of Madame Marbois was not good. He also pled valid business reasons for leaving, as he had inherited property and was suffering losses through his absence.

Marbois said the profound difference of opinion between him and Chilleau made it impossible for him to be of further service in the colony.[31] He was especially provoked by Chilleau's decision to remove some of the restrictions on foreign commerce, because of a shortage of provisions and exorbitant prices. Both men agreed that something should be done, but they favored radically different remedies. Marbois thought two to three thousand barrels of flour at each of the main ports—Le Cap, Port-au-Prince, and Les Cayes—would be quite sufficient, and he proposed to grant the right of importing the flour to certain designated merchants in each city. The governor insisted on a complete suspension of the regulation forbidding the importation of foreign flour, but Marbois did persuade him to limit the order to three months, beginning March 31, 1789.[32] An even more serious disagreement soon followed. Chilleau decided to encourage the backward south by opening it to foreign commerce. He exceeded his powers, but there was a good deal of common sense in his action, since French shipping supplied that section very inadequately. Marbois stood firmly by the law, as behooved a good administrator, and vigorously opposed the governor.

Decrees of the governor and intendant were registered in the colony by the Superior Council in the same fashion that decrees of the King were registered by the Parlement of Paris. When an act to open the southern ports for five years was presented by the governor, Marbois not only refused to sign it but declared he would consider it invalid even after registry by the Council.[33] The decree was registered on May 11, and the break between the two administrators was complete. It was a weary man who now asked for permission to leave the colony as soon as possible. "The crisis in which I find myself personally is worse than I can describe. It is such that I would leave for France tomorrow (and you would approve) if I did not think it necessary to remain at my post until the last minute. The break between M. Chilleau and me is so profound that I entreat you to obtain my recall from His Majesty. If the pretended ordinance is confirmed, do not leave me here a minute, Monseigneur. I consider the system the ruin of a fifth of the realm, and my opinion on this point is unchangeable."[34]

The five or six months he would have to wait for a reply to his letter seemed longer to Marbois than all the time he had already spent in St. Domingue. The suppression of the Council at Le Cap had turned the north against him, and his opposition to the new ordinance would embitter the south. Only the west, particularly the city of Port-au-Prince, was at all favorable to his policies. When the governor desired to prolong the free entry of flour another three months, Marbois, after refusing his consent, absented himself from the session of the Council where the decree was registered.[35] The tension proved trying for Chilleau also, especially since he realized he had exceeded his authority. He wrote on June 20 that Marbois opposed him so vigorously he was coming to France on July 10 or 15 to defend his cause, and that of the colony. He added that one object of his trip was the recall of Marbois, with whom he found it impossible to carry on the administration.[36]

On May 22, Luzerne presented Marbois' request to the King's Council but stated that he felt it would be injurious to the royal service to allow the intendant to leave the colony. Yet, since he had been away ten years it was difficult to refuse. The minister therefore suggested that Marbois be asked to remain as long as possible but be allowed to take a year's leave of absence if he felt it advisable.[37] He wrote his friend as follows: "His Majesty, to whom I reported your request, who knows and approves your zeal and your actions, permits you, though with regret, to return next April. But he would prefer that you not use this permission . . . I enclose the leave of absence which I submit to your discretion."[38]

In France the King's Council applauded Marbois' stand and annulled the ordinance throwing the south open to foreign commerce. A stern letter was sent to the Superior Council blaming it for failing to show the governor he had exceeded his powers. Only in urgent cases where the defense of the colony was at stake could the governor act without the consent of the intendant.[39] Chilleau was recalled and, as he had already left the colony when the order arrived, he was later refused an audience by Louis XVI. The King said he could not receive a military official who had deserted his post, unless such a person had been exonerated by a council of war.[40] Louis XVI added a postscript in his own hand to Luzerne's letter commending Marbois: "It is by my explicit order that M. Luzerne is writing you. Continue to fulfill your functions and be as useful to me as you have been up to now. You may be sure of my approbation and esteem and you may count on my good will."[41] When Peinier, the new governor, arrived bringing the King's approval of Marbois' conduct, the intendant was overcome with joy and his heart was so melted that he said kind things of the former governor, "one whose weakness had been a desire to favor the colonists." Marbois prepared to spend several more years in St. Domingue.[42]

But the intendant's real troubles were just beginning, and events of the next few months made the quarrel with Chilleau look like a tempest in a teapot. St. Domingue now experienced the first shock of that French revolutionary movement which was destined to change the world. Not even Paris itself was affected so profoundly as the rich island of the Caribbean. By 1795 a whole civilization was destroyed, the planters dead or in exile, and the prosperity of the island gone forever. From the chaos a remarkable negro, Toussaint L'Ouverture, began the construction of a new society, but he fell before the treachery of Napoleon, and St. Domingue lapsed into barbarism.

There were three stages in the revolution which destroyed the *ancien régime* in St. Domingue. The colonials undermined and overthrew the authority of the existing government just as the opposition did in France. Then the mulattoes rose against the planters, and, finally, the slaves rose against all the rest. Marbois fell a victim to the first uprising, for to the colonials he was the soul of all they detested in the old government.

While all France was discussing what an Estates General would be like after 175 years and speculating on its functions, some adventuresome spirits in St. Domingue began to clamor for representation of the island in that body. Luzerne had instructed Chilleau to prevent agitation on the subject and the convocation of any assemblies for choosing deputies until the Estates General itself could decide whether the colonies should be represented.[43] On December 5, 1788, the Chamber of Agriculture at Le Cap presented a memoir asking admission of deputies from the colony in the Estates General. The petition caused quite a sensation, including a good deal of opposition. The governor and the intendant merely forwarded the document to France without taking any stand on the matter.[44] The pressure of the colonists increased, however, and the governor and intendant, being then without instructions, allowed the leaders to go ahead. Marbois later avowed that he was opposed to the elections, but "we put no obstacle in the way of the elections which the inhabitants held on their own initiative." Some four thousand people took part, and thirteen deputies were chosen.[45] These deputies followed a radical policy in Paris and were ardent supporters of the Third Estate in its successful campaign to unite the three orders in a National Assembly.

The deputies were hostile to Marbois, and they presented a unanimous request for "the immediate recall of the Intendant Marbois, justly abhorred by St. Domingue, which for three years has urgently and vainly solicited his recall."[46] The memoir was given to the King on July 30 and he asked Luzerne to prepare a report for the Council, which was presented on August 13. The minister stated that Marbois' conduct was in strict conformity with the law, but, as he had himself expressed a desire to leave St. Domingue, it would be easy to satisfy the colonists by permitting him to use immediately the leave of absence he had received for the next spring.[47]

The Council approved a letter which Luzerne had prepared on August 10, stating that Louis XVI's regard for Marbois was unchanged but that "in the present circumstances it is difficult for him to sustain one of the persons by whom he had been best served." ("The present circumstances" were the fall of the Bastille and the grave disorders that swept over northern and eastern France in July and August, 1789.) Marbois was told that it was to the interest of the King that he make prompt use of the leave which formerly had been left to his discretion. On the same day, in addressing Peinier, the new governor, the minister observed forebodingly: "Never has a more general agitation reigned [in France]. It is to be feared that it will spread into our distant possessions, and especially to the flourishing colony you command. . . . Try to preserve the richest and most important of its colonies for the Mother Country. This should be your principal aim." The minister added that he feared for Marbois' safety, if the general effervescence of France should communicate itself to St. Domingue. In such a case Peinier was asked to take special pains to protect him.[48] A general order from Versailles to all colonial governors and intendants permitting the admission of foreign flour for six months is eloquent testimony of the disintegration of the system Marbois was endeavoring to defend.[49]

In the colony there was a lull before the terrible storm of revolt. By September 25, the news of events in Paris through July 20 had arrived in Port-au-Prince, but the governor and intendant were able to report that the King's authority was respected as it should be. They were forced, however, to wink at the publication of pamphlets describing the uprising of Paris and the capitulation of the monarch and the National Assembly before it. The question which haunted them at night was the same that hangs eternally over lands populated by blacks dominated by a handful of whites—the fear of race war. The possibility of an outbreak was rendered more likely by the barbarities of some planters in handling their slaves.[50]

Two weeks later all was quiet at Port-au-Prince, but serious agitation had begun in the north. The old enmity against the intendant because of his rigorous administration and the suppression of the Superior Council at Le Cap was rekindled by news of the abolition of privilege and most feudal dues in France on August 9 and 10. "All that part of the government which is purely administrative has received serious setbacks. Everyone tries to profit from the situation."[51] The officials avoided taking the new national cockade of blue, white, and red for ten or twelve days, but when they heard of the enthusiasm with which it was taken at Le Cap, they put it on themselves. Marbois had cockades prepared for the officers and men, and his wife distributed them.

The wild young men at Le Cap had already condemned their enemy in the best *sans culotte* fashion. A group of them met on September 21, declared the intendant guilty of various civil charges—refusal to allow flour to enter the colony, for example—and ordered him "to be hanged and strangled until his death from a gallows erected on the Place de Clugny of this city . . . . then his body burned, his ashes thrown to the wind, and his goods confiscated for the use of the poor of the colony."[52] Marbois' recall was announced and placards appeared proposing his assassination and the burning of his house. In view of the steadily mounting disorders, Peinier and Marbois appealed to the minister for the issuance of a declaration by the National Assembly, saying the old officials were to remain in power until the government of the island could be considered at Versailles.[53]

Luzerne's letter, which snatched him from a horrible fate, must have appeared providential to Marbois. There is little doubt that the statement in his memoirs that he was reluctant to go is less than half truth. Braver men than he would not have hesitated to flee the danger that threatened. The minister's letter arrived on October 19, and Marbois sailed on the night of October 26. The intendant's leaving was in keeping with his character. He put his accounts in order and published them.[54] Then he left a long, printed memoir for the use of his successor, giving him much advice obviously intended as a public vindication of himself and a reprimand for his critics. There were a million livres in the treasury, not counting certain sums belonging to particular institutions. He urged his successor to construct roads and bridges, erect fountains, and provide running water for the cities.[55] This was something more than a gesture, for Marbois wrote Vincent privately on October 19 that he hoped the great public works undertaken during his administration would be finished. The necessary funds to complete the road from Port-au-Prince to Jacmel and from Gonaives to Le Cap were on hand.[56]

On October 26, Marbois presided at the Superior Council for the last time. It was with emotion that he announced his departure and that he made his last visit to the government hospitals. That evening a group of friends were calling on the intendant when a special messenger arrived announcing the approach of a deputation from Le Cap. For some time reports had circulated that a group of five hundred young men in the north were going to march on Port-au-Prince and seize Marbois. The governor sent 150 troops to meet the marchers, and as the result of a hurried conference Marbois and his family decided to depart that very evening rather than the next day, as originally planned.[57]

"Everything was ready by sundown, and at nine o'clock, taking leave of our friends, my family and I accompanied by the General [Governor] went to the sea shore. The launches awaited us. Our children, astonished by the sobbing of their nurses, whom it was necessary to leave behind, by the sight of the sea, and by the novelty of this happening during their ordinary bed time, attracted everyone in hearing distance by their crying. A crowd soon collected. I embraced those who were my friends. My wife and I, each taking a child in our arms, boarded the launch. It left the land [and] we were soon in the open sea. United to all I held dearest in the world I had no feeling of bitterness, but was happy to be my own master again."[58] The family boarded the *Ariel,* a government vessel, and said farewell to St. Domingue forever.

Peinier's judgment of Marbois was eminently fair. He pronounced his departing colleague a splendid administrator and a master of economy, but tactless in his dealings with the public. "He leaves a host of enemies in the colony, his person would be unsafe here if he remained, yet one cannot take a step without encountering some trace of the good he has done. The enthusiasm, the ability, and the virtue he practices in both public and private life make me deplore sincerely the unfortunate circumstances which led to his recall. It is an irreparable loss for the colony."[59] Marbois' departure was mourned by the slaves, as he had done all he could to see that they were treated humanely. In 1818, a negro senator was found cherishing the intendant's carriage as his most prized possession.[60]

The intendant had been advised by friends in St. Domingue to go to Philadelphia and remain at the home of his father-in-law until normal conditions returned in France.[61] As he advanced toward Paris from Spain, where he had landed at Cadiz on December 3,[62] he felt the fears of his associates were groundless. The merchants of Bayonne and Bordeaux who had profited by his strict enforcement of commercial regulations gave him the welcome he deserved. But he soon found the atmosphere in Paris quite different. The planters resident there regarded both him and Luzerne as negrophiles and through the Club de Massaic had levied thirteen accusations against them. Fortunately Marbois had brought the papers essential for exonerating his regime, and he now prepared a memoir which refuted his detractors.[63] The opposition to him was so serious, however, that he decided to wait until the end of April before taking his family to Metz. The delay was a great disappointment as he had not seen his mother since his departure for America eleven years before, and she had never met his wife and the two children.

The charges Marbois combatted covered most of his years in the colony. The road to Le Cap was said to have been unnecessary and a source of graft. He and Luzerne were attacked for levying *corvées* of slave labor. This displeased the planters, who lost the labor, and also the humanitarians in France, who considered it barbarity out of keeping with the age. On the controversy with Chil-

leau, Marbois answered that there had never been a shortage of flour and that during the greatest scarcity he had
purchased flour at 132 livres the barrel and sold it for 120.
To the ridiculous charge that he had accumulated a stock
of flour in Philadelphia with his father-in-law for sale in
the colony, he replied that Mr. Moore had been retired
from business for twelve years. As a *grand coup* he reminded his critics that St. Domingue, according to Necker,
was the only colony not a burden to the state.

Occasional criticisms of his intendancy plagued Marbois during 1790. The National Assembly decreed that all
administrators submit their accounts, which Marbois did.
When one of his enemies at Le Cap, Monsieur de la Cheva-
lerie, questioned their accuracy, Marbois cited the published report of his successor, which showed that he found
over a million livres in the treasury and adequate provisions of all kinds.[64] Marbois' letter of defense was applauded when read in the National Assembly. Two other
communications from Marbois on St. Domingue are interesting primarily because of the change in his name.[65] "De
Marbois" would make his fortune no longer. Like the
forget-me-nots of Woippy, it belonged to the long ago. For
the moment plain "Barbé" came into its own again. That
was a name in keeping with *liberté, égalité, fraternité.*

CHAPTER V

The Plight of a Moderate in the French Revolution

FOR five years Barbé's private and public life was determined by the course of the French Revolution. Every major phase of this great upheaval after 1790 is reflected in his career. His fortunes and misfortunes show the course of the Revolution in both national and local affairs. Through him one sees what really happened to an upper-middle-class official who remained in France throughout the most violent phases of the bitter conflict.

Barbé's return from St. Domingue coincided with one of the calmest periods of the Revolution. The King and the Assembly had moved to Paris the preceding October, and Lafayette and the National Guard were keeping order in the capital. The representatives of the nation were free to concentrate upon the establishment of a constitution and the inauguration of a new administration.

Barbé had rendered such an excellent account of his work in St. Domingue that he was considered for a position in the new civil service. The National Assembly confiscated the royal property on May 9, 1790, and a month later voted the King an annual income of approximately $5,000,000, which was to be expended under the direction of a new official, the Intendant of the Civil List. Barbé was suggested for the post. He missed the appointment, according to his own story, because he insisted on the publication of accounts and refused to set aside a million dollars annually to bribe the press and members of the Assembly. His proposals were labeled "from the school of Necker" and rejected.[1] As the individual who received the office eventually died on the guillotine, Barbé had good reason to rejoice that he had not obtained the nomination.

As soon as he had secured himself from the attacks on his administration in St. Domingue, he took his family to Metz and settled down to the life of a country gentleman on the estate at Buchy, approximately twelve miles from the city, which he had owned before he went to America. In 1817, Buchy was a village of thirty-five houses, with a population of 184 people.[2] Since the number of houses remained the same in 1844 and the population had increased only one person,[3] there is reason to believe that these descriptions would have fitted the village equally well for 1791. The land of the village amounted to 1,055 acres, of which more than 852 were in cultivation and the remainder in forest. When the author visited Buchy in the summer of 1937, the village seemed to have changed very little in the past century. The forest, however, is gone, as Barbé cut the timber some time after 1807. The chateau, a substantial three-story building probably dating from the early eighteenth century, dominates the cottages of the peasants grouped around the church. The interior of the chateau suggests the frugality of the *bourgeoisie* rather than the

73

splendor of the nobility; no fine staircases or splendid ceilings ever adorned its simplicity. The house is in excellent condition and externally gives little evidence of change since the Barbé family occupied it.[4]

During 1790–91 Barbé devoted himself almost entirely to the management of his estate and the study of agriculture. He had a particular interest in the agricultural revolution just beginning in France, and he made a special study of the cultivation of clover. The growth of leguminous crops so fascinated him that he made a number of trips in the province to observe their cultivation and wrote a volume on clover, alfalfa, and sainfoin,[5] which was crowned by the departmental authorities at Metz.

The most significant event of 1791 in France was the attempted flight of Louis XVI. By spring the monarch had lost all sympathy for the revolution and awaited an opportunity to flee from his semi-captivity in Paris to the loyal troops on the eastern frontier. These were commanded by the Marquis de Bouillé, an acquaintance of Barbé, and an important detachment of his troops was stationed at Metz. The daring attempt ended in tragedy on June 21 when Louis XVI was recognized by a village postmaster, arrested at Varennes, and returned to the capital, where the National Assembly suspended him from the throne until September. The flight had seriously compromised the cause of constitutional monarchy.

It was only by accident that Barbé escaped direct implication in the ill-fated venture. Bouillé called at his home and talked vaguely of impending events of importance in which Barbé might assist. Bouillé tried to dissuade his host from

A Portion of
St Domingue

from a Map of 1796

LA TORTUE (Tortuga or Tortula)

Tortuga Channel

LE CAP FRANÇAIS

Port Paix

Jean Rabel

C. St Nicholas

Cap à Foux

Limits between the Spaniards and the French

PORT AU PRINCE

Port au Prince Bay

LA GOXAVE

LES COMITES

LES CAYES

Cap Dame Marie

WINDWARD PASSAGE

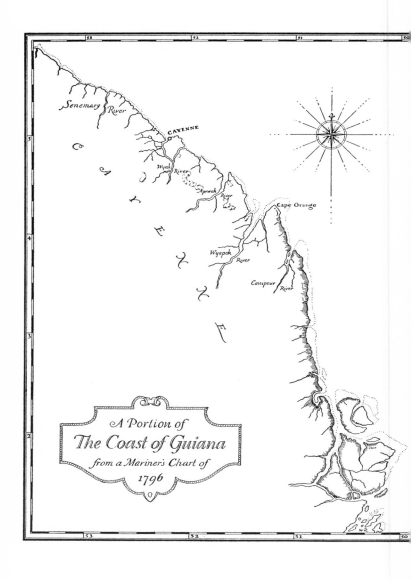

Senemary River

CAYENNE

C A Y

Wyah River

Aprwah River

Cape Orange

Wyapok River

Casipour River

E

A Portion of
The Coast of Guiana
from a Mariner's Chart of
1796

a projected journey to Switzerland, but as he refused to be more specific Barbé continued with his plans. His old friend and patron, Castries, had emigrated to Ouchy, Switzerland, and Barbé was preparing to visit him. As soon as he arrived at Castries' lodgings, he saw that the *émigrés* gathered there were much excited at the prospect of a significant event in France.

At the news of the King's flight they all set off for Coblenz, where they expected a new French government to be organized. Barbé then realized that the purpose of Bouillé's visit had been to solicit assistance for the King. He would doubtless have coöperated had the commandant revealed the purpose of his call. Castries and his friends, including Barbé, were on the road for France when a courier arrived from Madame Bouillé announcing the capture of the King at Varennes and his return to Paris. When Barbé determined to continue, despite this news, all his companions, save Castries, addressed him in insulting language. He returned to Buchy, however, without any difficulty.[6]

The Barbés lived quietly that summer and autumn but on November 2, 1791, their home was saddened by the death of their younger daughter, Elizabeth Laura, then a little over three years old. The blow was a heavy one from which the family never recovered.

After the return of Louis XVI to Paris, the Assembly hurried to complete the constitution begun at Versailles more than two years before. The responsible leaders realized that their best chance of restoring stability lay in promulgation of the constitution and the return of Louis XVI to the throne. The King accepted the constitution on September 14, the Legislative Assembly met on October 1, and the cry went up, "the Revolution is over." Barbé fervently hoped it was true. He approved of the constitution, though he hoped to amend it in order to strengthen the executive. It was with pleasure, therefore, that he accepted an invitation to enter the diplomatic service of the new government.

Revolutionary France had come into sharp conflict with the states of the Holy Roman Empire. The Legislative Assembly was incensed by the hospitality accorded French *émigrés* in the Rhineland. The Elector of Trèves, particularly, was accused of aiding the *émigrés'* plans against the revolutionary government. The Empire was aroused by the property losses which the Alsatian nobles suffered through the abolition of most feudal dues in France on the famous evening of August 4–5, 1789. Alsace, previously the personal possession of the French King, had been made an integral part of France by the National Assembly and subjected to the new, confiscatory decrees. Most important of all, the revolutionaries feared that the Emperor would use these matters as an excuse for intervening in behalf of his sister, Marie Antoinette, suppressing the Constitution of 1791, and restoring the *ancien régime*.

Barbé's previous experience fitted him for the post of Minister to the Diet and special envoy to Austria, to which he was appointed at the end of 1791. His instructions envisaged a change in France's relations with the Diet, where little of significance had been enacted in generations. De Lessart, the foreign minister, contemplated the organization of the smaller German states as a third power in the Empire and thus a check on Austria and Prussia—somewhat the kind of system later erected by Napoleon. It was felt that France's neglect of the states of the Empire since her alliance with Austria in 1756 had been a fundamental mistake. Hitherto, the revolutionary government had lacked the courage to rid itself of the old diplomats and to embark on a new and aggressive policy of coöperation with the Diet. Marbois was to point out to the lesser states that the recent alliance of Austria and Prussia menaced them as well as France. He should invite the German princes to Paris for a discussion of the land problems that had arisen from the abolition of feudalism in Alsace. Marbois was warned, however, that the alliance with Austria still held, and he was instructed not to antagonize the ministers of the Hapsburgs.[7]

Despite these written instructions, the most important part of Marbois' mission was the trip to Vienna, which preceded the journey to Ratisbon. Louis XVI was still served by ministers who desired the maintenance of peace with Austria. De Lessart decided to send Marbois to reassure Leopold II about the Revolution and the pacific intentions of France. Before leaving, the new envoy requested audiences with the King and Queen. The interview with Louis XVI revealed all too clearly the lack of decision which doomed that incompetent ruler to the guillotine. Marbois told the monarch that he had been instructed to assure Austria that France desired peace and he requested an assurance that this was the sentiment of the King. Louis XVI answered evasively and ended by telling the minister to conform to his instructions.

The audience with the Queen occurred in secrecy at ten in the evening. Marie Antoinette leaned against the mantle and spoke with that vigor which has led a modern historian to describe her as "the only man at the Court." She was animated and talked frankly of foreign affairs and her own personal dangers. She professed love for her brother, the late Joseph II, but admitted distrust of her brother, Leopold II, who had succeeded him. "He will deceive you if he can, there is not in all Italy[8] a falser man than he." She told Marbois she desired peace, and she appeared much more conscious than her husband of the concessions that must be made to the Revolution.[9] The Queen announced that she feared to give Marbois letters for the Viennese court but that she was sending them via Brussels[10] and was sure they would precede him.

Marbois took the oath as minister to Ratisbon on January 20[11] and hurried to Vienna, bearing a passport signed by the King, De Lessart, Pétion, Mayor of Paris, and Dietrich, Mayor of Strasbourg—all of whom met violent deaths in the course of the Revolution. He saw Lafayette at Metz and found him enthusiastic for a war against Austria. The journey through Germany was somewhat in the nature of a homecoming, and Marbois saw old friends in Strasbourg, Karlsruhe, Stuttgart, and Munich. Nearly everywhere he found an ill-concealed delight at the internal commotion which reduced the power of France in foreign affairs. Most of the courts felt that Louis XVI would be able to reassert his authority eventually. The Emperor seemed most troubled by the fact that he had to maintain troops in the Low Countries, where a revolt had just been suppressed, at a cost of 1,500,000 florins a month. Marbois considered Prussia the villain of the piece and the only German power that desired war with France.[12]

Marbois arrived in Vienna on February 10. The letter he carried from De Lessart to the Duc de Noailles, the French Minister at Vienna, described him as "enlightened, wise, of excellent principles, and filled with enthusiasm for the service of the king." Noailles was told that "the information M. de Marbois can give you verbally will explain our actual position and our wishes." Marbois brought assurances of French desire for peace. He was ordered to find out the real views of the court on the losses of the Alsatian princes and to tell the Austrian government that any proposals contrary to the new French Constitution would be rejected peremptorily.[13]

Noailles took Marbois at once to see Kaunitz, the foreign minister, who received him so coldly that the two Frenchmen departed immediately. A number of *émigrés* in the salon were exceedingly discourteous, and some of them openly snubbed Marbois. The following day Kaunitz received the letters of Marie Antoinette and he endeavored to make amends for his rudeness. The papal nuncio averred that the Austrian minister had been misled by the *émigrés,* who desired Austrian intervention in France. Leopold then received Marbois in an audience which the French minister thought was the last one the Emperor gave before his sudden death on March 1, 1792.[14] Leopold was succeeded by Francis, his eldest son.

Noailles, who had encountered considerable difficulty in making the aggressive action of the Legislative Assembly appear pacific, welcomed Marbois with open arms and at once arranged for him to discuss the points of irritation with the Prince of Colloredo, former tutor of Francis, and Count Cobentzel, the vice-chancellor of the Empire.[15] Marbois filed a long report of the latter conversation.[16] He felt the new Emperor, Francis II, would follow a reasonable course in the matter of the Alsatian princes. Cobentzel said that the powers of Europe could not recognize the annexation of the papal territory of Avignon by France, which had occurred in 1791, so long as the pope objected, but he intimated that an arrangement might be reached with the Vatican. Marbois felt no friend of the French constitution could complain of the vice-chancellor's attitude toward it and the power of the King. He did not think Austria had any serious interest in the *émigrés,* in fact, many Viennese opposed supporting a party which was attempting to upset the laws of a friendly state. Cobentzel showed a conciliatory spirit on the subject of armaments and promised that no further troops would be called. Austria would do nothing at Trèves or Mayence which might disturb France. Colloredo had been equally pacific, and Marbois felt if the words of these two reputedly honest ministers carried any weight there would be no war that year.

The Emperor planned to submit Louis XVI's reply concerning the Alsatian princes to the Diet, so De Lessart instructed Marbois to take up his residence at Ratisbon in time for the opening session. He was to follow the deliberations of the Diet at first hand and direct them as much as possible. De Lessart believed the Diet would be reasonable in the revision of the Alsatian boundary, and such a policy would enable the Legislative Assembly to make sacrifices for the maintenance of peace without compromising its principles or its prestige.[17] Marbois found considerable distrust of France among the princes at Ratisbon. They feared that the forces of the French Revolution, if unchecked, would threaten privilege throughout the continent. He sensed, however, that Germany would be happy to rid herself of the *émigrés*, who were keeping up a dangerous agitation. He also felt that many of the *émigrés* would gladly return home if they were reassured regarding their personal safety.[18]

The sudden death of Leopold produced an imperial interregnum which was expected to last until August. Francis' election was a foregone conclusion but the formalities required several months. In the meantime Marbois' credentials could not be accepted and the Diet would be largely inactive. Marbois had been given wide discretion as to his personal movements, and he decided to return to Paris until his presence in Ratisbon would be useful. He learned at Metz that a ministerial revolution had occurred at Paris, sweeping De Lessart from office.

The Revolution had just taken a major turn to the left. The two main groups in the Legislative Assembly were the Feuillants and the Girondins. The former were loyal supporters of the King and the Constitution of 1791. The latter were suspicious of the King and hostile to the constitution. At heart many of them were republicans, though they still rendered lip service to the monarchy. Hitherto the Feuillants had controlled the Assembly, but their power had declined steadily before the determined attack of their radical enemies. In March, Louis XVI was forced to recognize the situation by dismissing his Feuillant ministers and choosing a Girondin cabinet. The Girondins were a war party and very hostile to Austria.

Dumouriez, the new foreign minister, directed Marbois to come to Paris at once.[19] He was told that the new ministry at first regarded him as a member of the party that had betrayed the King by imprudent advice but that a reading of his dispatches had led them to change their opinion. He was instructed to return at once to Ratisbon, which would be the center of negotiations for all Germany. Marbois was not in sympathy with Dumouriez's policies, and he sought a safe way of resigning his position. He communicated his desire to Marie Antoinette through the Archbishop of Toulouse, saying he would remain if the crown really wished it. The Queen, however, placed no obstacle in the way of his resigning. "He should reserve himself for us and for another occasion," she said.[20] Dumouriez accepted his resignation in a curt note informing him that he would be replaced at once and asking an immediate return of his credentials.[21] He reminded Marbois that he was too prudent to need cautioning about secrecy concerning all that had been communicated to him. On April 20, 1792, France declared war on Francis as "King of Hungary and Bohemia." It was hoped that the other states of the Holy Roman Empire would remain neutral. Failure in the war soon brought the downfall of the monarchy. On August 10, 1792, a mob attacked the Tuileries and forced the royal family to flee to the Legislative Assembly. This body speedily suspended the monarch and called for the election of a National Convention to determine the permanent government for France. The Girondins took control when the new body met in September. A republic was proclaimed and Louis XVI tried for treason. The Girondins tried to prevent his execution but the more radical Jacobins forced the death penalty. Major defeats in the war in the spring of 1793 broke the Girondin power and placed the Jacobins at the helm by June. They soon inaugurated a systematic campaign of Terror which lasted until August, 1794. The outstanding Jacobin leader was Robespierre, who hoped to build a republic of virtue according to the principles of Rousseau.

In the years immediately following Barbé's resignation of the ministry to Ratisbon his family was sometimes at Metz and sometimes at the estate in Buchy. They encountered the dangers common to officials of the *ancien régime,* but despite the extreme violence of the Revolution at Metz, escaped without any serious threat to their lives. At first it seemed that Barbé would encounter little difficulty in adjusting himself to the life of the community, for he received an appointment as a commissioner for establishing the new land and personal property taxes in the department.[22] But the fall of the monarchy and the violence of the factions soon touched the Barbés' happiness. Strangely enough, Madame Barbé was first attacked. In August, 1792, she had planned a trip to Philadelphia to see her family and divide the property of her recently deceased father. Because of the war she found it impossible to embark from Holland, as she had planned, and thus returned to Metz. Five months thereafter she was accused of being an *émigré,* and the same charge was leveled against her husband on March 2, 1793.[23] He was arrested, put in prison, and seals placed on all his goods and papers. Two days later he was released but his papers were retained in order to see whether there was any evidence of his wife's emigration. Madame Barbé was then in hiding, and the seals were left on her personal goods. On March 11, the local committee removed Barbé's name from the list, but this was overlooked in Paris, a fact which led to the confiscation of his property in 1798. Barbé published a memoir in his wife's defense.

The decision turned on the question of her nationality; was she French or American? Madame Barbé appealed for assistance to Gouverneur Morris, the American minister, who certified that she was an American citizen.[24] He asked Lebrun, the minister of foreign affairs, to take up her case with the minister of the interior or the authorities of the department of the Moselle, in which Metz is located. Lebrun replied promptly that he had asked his colleague "to take measures compatible with the laws of the republic and the regard we always have for requests made by the representative of the United States of America." A fortnight later, however, Madame Barbé was still not absolved as an *émigré* and she wrote Morris again. The American minister assured her that he had taken steps in her favor and encouraged her to believe that the case would be settled any day. On April 25, 1793, the Metz Committee of Surveillance heard Madame Barbé's petition and decreed that "she could not be considered an *émigré* since she was not really French."[25] However, the departmental authorities who had jurisdiction over the municipal committee referred the question to the Executive Council in Paris, and no decision had been reached by August when Morris once again took the matter up with the foreign office. This time he tried to secure a decision by stating that the Moore family had expressed its wishes for the success of the French Revolution. Deforgues, the new minister, prepared a report for the Executive Committee and asked a definite decision immediately. The Committee referred the question again to the minister of the interior, who requested that Barbé write him on the subject. Morris then thought the matter settled, and he was amazed to learn more than three months later that no report had been made by the Executive Council. He comforted Madame Barbé with the observation that she would not be molested "because the system of persecution will be less rigidly pursued than heretofore."

The frequent changes in Paris, however, and their repercussions throughout the country left no peace of mind for men of Barbé's class. On January 25, 1794, one finds him again arrested and detained in his house at Buchy because of a decree of November 24, 1793, ordering the arrest of all former intendants. Barbé pointed out that the decree applied only to intendants in France and that his own accounts had been received and approved by the National Assembly. He cited testimonials by his neighbors that he was a good citizen and that he had never been known to do anything contrary to the laws of the Republic.[26] Apparently he was released in a few days and the charges dropped, but the incident well illustrates the confusion and uncertainty of the Terror. Seven months later his wife was still worried, for the fall of Robespierre a few days before had suspended the proceedings by which she expected to have her own case ended completely. As she wrote to Morris, "I experience the same anxiety at each change of administration in this department." The proofs of her innocence were all in Paris and she asked Morris to see whether he could secure a conclusion of the interrupted proceedings. If this were impossible she asked that he commend her cause to James Monroe, the new minister, who was about to arrive from America. She rejoiced in the fact that she and her husband had known Monroe in the United States. It is difficult to determine the final procedure in her case, but Madame Barbé was not troubled any more.

Barbé later described the 9 Thermidor, on which Robespierre fell, as "the day when rascals, fearing for their heads, resolved to cut off that of another rascal who menaced them,"[27] but it set in motion a train of events which brought the moderates to power in Paris and throughout the country. The National Convention purged the municipal administration at Metz, and a complete reaction set in against the twenty months of radicalism that had terrorized the city. Barbé was a leader of the moderate group and on January 25, Genevois, *représentant en mission* for the departments of the Moselle and the Meurthe, deposed Barthélemy, the mayor of Metz, and appointed Barbé in his stead.[28]

The new mayor, who had already been on a mission to Paris for the city, felt some reluctance about heading such a turbulent municipality. Genevois had appointed him without following the usual electoral forms, and Barbé

86

hesitated to undertake the office without a mandate from the leaders of the commune. He addressed a printed pamphlet to his fellow citizens setting forth his personal status and his views on public questions. His residence at Buchy during the past three years technically disqualified him for the office, but he expressed a willingness to undertake it if the commune desired it. He explained, however, that his program would be conservative: regular payment of taxes, order in the city, no more debts, severe economy, annual publication of accounts, no new construction, and no expensive amusements until the budget could be balanced.[29] The Council of the Commune elected him, and he accepted on February 25, though illness delayed his installation until March 3. His acceptance was couched in universal political language: "If I had known the good will of my fellow citizens toward me I would not have hesitated a moment to join you. The assurances you give me are more than I could expect. I no longer fear appearing a stranger to the inhabitants of this commune when the friends of the people and the magistrates of their choice guarantee the opposite."[30]

The problems Barbé faced were similar to those confronted by mayors of American cities during any great depression. The prime consideration was the maintenance of food for an impoverished population. Even in normal times the authorities of the *ancien régime* had found it difficult to supply all the nation with an adequate bread supply. Metz belonged to that third of France which produced less grain than it consumed, much of the land being in vineyards and forests. Before the Revolution the city had been filled with religious institutions dispensing charity, but the confiscation of ecclesiastical property forced the government to assume these obligations.[31]

The new mayor wrote on March 10 to Lepayen, an old friend and now a member of the Committee of Provisions for the Republic, beseeching a loan of 1,500,000 francs. Lepayen approved the request but it was held up by routine procedure in the Convention. Barbé wrote Lepayen on April 4 that he had received neither the money nor one thousand quintals of rice he had expected and that soon he would be without resources of any kind.[32] The result would be disorder and perhaps bloodshed in a city so filled with Jacobin memories. The mayor and council tried to curb the unruly elements by a proclamation on March 22, ordering the questioning, and even provisional arrest, of citizens spreading disastrous or alarming news in *cafés,* theaters, and other public places.[33]

Events soon showed that the fears of the moderates were well founded. In order to meet the food shortage Barbé had collected a quantity of potatoes in the city. He and the council also considered it advisable to raise the price of bread, purchased with the depreciated paper money (assignats) which had begun to fall again after the death of Robespierre. When the new price became known a great crowd assembled at the Hôtel de Ville. In his memoirs Barbé gives a colorful account of what happened. At 6:00 A. M. on April 15, he went to his desk wearing the full regalia of his office. The crowd outside was yelling against the rise in the price of bread. Soon the councilors joined him, and the people flowed into the public council chamber

88

calling for the mayor to repeal the decree. The national guard rushed to defend the officials but Barbé took the gun from the most advanced guardsman and asked the officer to withdraw the men. For the moment this produced a good effect, but when the mayor tried to speak the audience howled him down by telling him to read the Declaration of the Rights of Man hanging behind his desk. At this point some women attacked a woman who had a loaf of bread just purchased at the new price. They were strangling her when the mayor, assisted by another woman, got her safely into a neighboring room. He then addressed the crowd: "Citoyennes, one of you has just helped me save an innocent person, let her come and receive from me the fraternal accolade." He kissed the woman and gave her a handful of assignats. Again the fickle crowd wavered toward the mayor, who now polled the council on the maintenance of the new price. Barbé says the majority were doubtful but he did not hesitate to announce "the new price remains." A sudden volley of potatoes was loosed at his head from all sides. "Repeal your decree," the mob shouted, "here are your potatoes." A woman cried, "Push his chair against his legs, he will fall, and we will finish him." But the mob was not murderous, and this would-be leader found no followers. At this point a note was handed the mayor reporting the approach of troops. Barbé feared the results of a clash with the military, so he pretended to read an announcement of disturbance in the third ward of the city requiring his presence and calmly left the scene.[34] The disorder had lasted two hours.

The official records confirm part of Barbé's story and

do not contradict any of it.[35] The agent of the national government reëstablished the old price provisionally and the council decided to maintain this suspension of the decree which had caused all the tumult. J. B. D. Mazade, the *représentant en mission* in the departments of the Moselle and the Meurthe, issued a decree the same day ordering the troops at Metz to support the commune and to arrest certain individuals responsible for the incident. He commended the mayor and the national agent for "the courage with which they defended and saved a citizen from the cowardly and bloody hands of assassins."[36]

Again the city protested its needs to Paris: "We foresee terrible evils if the Convention does not come promptly to our rescue. You know this country; once depleted by the deliveries made to the armies, it is without resources in the environs. . . . At Paris, apparently, they do not appreciate the frightful condition of a commune inhabited by 40,000 people of whom 34,000 receive their food by the efforts of the authorities. The potatoes which have nourished them up to now are about exhausted, and if we do not receive aid 34,000 people will starve to death."[37] Barbé reported on April 27 that the city was quiet for the moment, but he saw no way of avoiding disorder before the harvest unless they were assisted. Paris responded by allowing the city to take one thousand quintals of rice from the military stores in Metz. The mayor wrote Lepayen on May 5 that the city was supplied and all went well again.[38]

The day following the "potato riot" the municipality ordered the publication of a financial statement lauding the recovery of the city under Barbé's administration and calling upon the people to maintain order. The bookkeeping was of that ingenious variety which sets up an ordinary and an emergency budget. The first was reported balanced. "No longer does one announce that he is quitting the service of the commune, refusing to work for it, or ceasing to furnish its daily needs. Our fountains, long dry, flow again. Our streets are passable. The bodies of seven hundred dead animals scattered around our walls have just been buried in deep ditches, and the air is purified. You hear no longer the groans of your creditors; we summon them by the public papers."[39] The prosperity of the city, so the report stated, depended upon the suppression of that small minority which detested economy and order in public business.

The moderates remained firmly in control in the spring and summer and on August 31 the authorities felt strong enough to suppress the *Société Populaire,* the leading radical organization in the city.[40] The mayor was evidently reassured about the future, for he took occasion to invite James Monroe to visit him and Madame Barbé in their home.[41] A few weeks later, however, Barbé was deposed from his functions.

The removal of Barbé as mayor is still somewhat of a mystery. Undoubtedly his conservative administration had stirred up the *sans culottes,* but it is impossible today to be sure on what charges he was dismissed. He himself asserted that no reason was ever given for his removal.[42] On October 14, he received a decree of the Legislative Committee of the Convention saying he had been dismissed on the request of a deputation from the department of Moselle. The commune decreed the following day that it knew of no motive for Barbé's disgrace. The department issued a similar statement. The district of Metz praised the former mayor as one who "united in an eminent degree that spirit of order, economy, foresight, and punctuality without which administration is only chaos." Despite this disgrace other events were bringing Barbé into national influence.

After the death of Robespierre the conservative middle class assumed control of the National Convention. The surviving Girondin deputies were recalled and the Jacobin clubs suppressed. A new republican constitution was drafted and approved in a national plebiscite. The dying Convention decreed that two thirds of the new bicameral legislature should come from its own members, since the revolutionaries feared for both themselves and the nation should there be a complete change in government personnel. This extremely unpopular act laid the basis for the most serious friction in the new assemblies.

Elections for the remaining third of the legislature were held in the autumn and on October 10 Barbé was named an elector for the canton of Metz. Voting was indirect. The taxpayers first chose electors in the local districts and these met as an assembly to select the officials of the department. Barbé was made secretary for the sessions at the initial meeting of the assembly for the department of the Moselle on October 13. Three deputies were to be chosen from the department. In the balloting, which began on October 17, Pecheur received 256 votes and Barbé 198 from a possible 288, and they were at once declared elected. Their future colleague, Thiébaut, was chosen on the second ballot by a vote of only 156.[43]

Barbé's election was unpopular with the radicals and efforts had been made to discredit him in August when the *Journal des Hommes Libres* in Paris had revived the old charges about St. Domingue and had also accused him of returning to France with the Prussian invaders in 1792.[44] Later he was named the author of the Declaration of Pillnitz of 1791, in which Austria and Prussia had called on the powers of Europe to restrain the French Revolution. This rumor also reached Paris, where the *Journal du Matin* used it as a text for recounting the former mayor's alleged perfidies. He was accused of persecuting *patriotes,* provoking murder in a speech on 9 Thermidor, and of being an enemy of the Republic: "The words 'republic' and 'liberty' have never been soiled by his vile and servile lips." Barbé was labeled as "the soul of the counter-revolutionaries in the department of the Moselle." The author concluded by hoping that "like the gnat he would burn himself in the candle and that all his diplomatic ruses would shatter on the irremovable rock of liberty."[45]

This typical revolutionary attack might be ignored, but Barbé could not disregard the repetition of the Pillnitz charge made before the Convention by Tallien, one of the leaders in the overthrow of Robespierre. While Barbé was en route to Paris, the Convention printed Tallien's report and sent it to the departments and the army. Barbé challenged his detractors on his arrival and produced decrees of the commune of Metz and the department of the Moselle proving his innocence. He insisted that the new legislature investigate the charge and vindicate his conduct. Barbé's defense was read before the new lower house, where the charges had been repeated. Genevois, who had appointed him mayor and was now a member of this body, defended Barbé warmly: "During my mission in the Department of the Moselle," he reported, "I heard a great number of citizens render homage to the patriotic principles of Barbé-Marbois and to the conduct he followed during the time he was mayor of Metz. The inhabitants of this city often gave me the best reports of him." Tallien was summoned to present the proofs of his accusation, but he managed to avoid this impossible task, and Barbé pressed for an exoneration. This time the lower house passed over the issue by saying that the charge had been made originally in the newspapers and that the accused should seek redress from them.[46] Barbé had really won a public vindication. He thought the horrors of the revolution were behind him, but in fact the most terrifying experiences of his life lay ahead.

CHAPTER VI

Deportation to Guiana by the Directory

IN the organization of the new French government Barbé became a member of the Council of Ancients, the upper house, which was supposed to supply wisdom and restraint to the imagination of the younger men in the Five Hundred. The Ancients were required to be at least forty years old, and married men or widowers. The new executive consisted of five men, known as the Directory, chosen by the two houses of the legislature, one Director retiring each year. In popular parlance the name of the executive was applied to all divisions of the new government, and the republican regime of 1795 to 1799 is known to history as "the Directory."

A change in Barbé's name, significant of the times, occurred with his entry into national politics. The new constitution was the work of conservative men of property and a far cry from the radicalism of 1793. The revival of "Marbois" was safe and fashionable, so former mayor Barbé became legislator Barbé-Marbois. He continued to write his name in this hyphenated fashion until his elevation to the nobility, and it is as "Barbé-Marbois" that he is remembered today.

In the Ancients, Barbé-Marbois soon associated himself with such men as Charles-François-Lebrun, Royer-Collard, Dupont de Nemours, Portalis, Siméon, Tronçon-Ducoudray, and their leader Mathieu Dumas.[1] This group exercised a great influence in the choice of presidents and secretaries and in the nomination of commissions.[2] The new third in the legislature generally followed its leadership. The historian Thiers describes Barbé-Marbois and his friends as "not those extraordinary men who shine at the outset of revolutions, but men of solid merit, who succeed genius in the career of politics as in that of the arts."[3] Madelin regards them as "prudent men very much averse to adventurous undertakings."[4] They were generally more prosperous than their colleagues from the Convention. About a dozen of the new members met once or twice a week at the home of Barbé-Marbois or Gilbert Desmolières in the Rue de Clichy, and thus soon became known as the Clichiens.[5]

Barbé-Marbois and his intimates were men of moderate opinion inclined to censure but forgive the past and willing to support republican institutions.[6] Very few of them were royalists and Barbé-Marbois was certainly not one of these. With the passing of the Terror he had come to consider a moderate republic as the most sensible government for France. The Clichiens respected the constitution, hoping to secure control of the government through succeeding elections. In the meantime, they directed their criticism at the Directory, which represented the views of the revolutionary majority in the chambers.

The new third maintained a biting but ineffectual attack on the executive, steadily widening the breach between the older and the newer elements in the government. The Directory was accused of corruption, criticized for its appointments, held responsible for the poor state of the finances, and charged with declaring war without consulting the legislative bodies. The Directory in turn charged the Councils with desiring the assassination of *patriotes* and the return of priests and *émigrés*. The legislature was said to be paralyzing the Directory by refusing to vote credits and by opposing peace.[7]

In this verbal battle of much distortion and some truth, Barbé-Marbois took an active part, insisting always that the letter of the constitution be enforced. He vigorously opposed a resolution allowing the Directory to appoint judges and administrators provisionally until elections could be held in the respective departments.[8] He proposed that the Directory furnish the Ancients with a statement of the finances of the Republic and keep them continually informed on all matters of importance.[9] His resolution for the nomination of a committee of nine to request information on agriculture, industry, commerce, colonies, navigation, population, the army and navy, revenue, expenses, debts, and national resources was considered premature by the majority of the Ancients. He deplored the speed with which laws were rushed through the Five Hundred and then presented to the Ancients under the plea of emergency,[10] and he opposed a reorganization of the navy, proposed by the Directory, which would place the administrative staff under the command of the naval officers.[11]

Barbé-Marbois' literary ability and his interest in arts and sciences were also of service at this time. The report on education which he submitted to the Ancients on March 20, 1796, is an invaluable analysis of the effect of the Revolution on the schools. The occasion was a competition inaugurated, but not completed, by the Convention for the purpose of determining what primary schoolbooks should be printed at state expense. He declared that teaching and learning had declined during the past five years, and that the Revolution had destroyed both the good and the bad in the schools of the nation. The schoolhouses in the rural districts were described as wretched affairs, poorly lighted, with leaky roofs, and often without floors. The masters were so poorly paid that they had to eke out an existence by engaging in some supplementary enterprise, usually agriculture. The rural schools were said to be serving only half the number of children taught in 1789, but the situation was somewhat better in the cities. Higher education was extinct except at Paris, where the Collège de France and the École Polytechnique endeavored vainly to cope with the demands of the nation.[12]

Despite periods of violence, the French Revolution had protected the right of private property. The middle-class leaders of the Revolution were therefore much alarmed by the doctrines of one Nicholas Babeuf, who openly advocated an economic and social revolution. Babeuf was accused of a conspiracy to overthrow the Directory, and he and a number of his followers were put to death.

The Babeuf plot brought a *rapprochement* between the new third and the Directory which lasted for eight months, until November, 1796, but it failed to effect a permanent reconciliation between the warring factions. Barbé-Marbois joined with his colleagues from the Moselle in a letter to their constituents explaining the arrest of Babeuf and accusing him of a plot to overthrow the existing government and restore the Jacobin Constitution of 1793. "The papers seized leave no doubt on this subject," they wrote. The letter was printed and distributed by the municipal authorities at Metz as a method of rallying the citizens "to the constitution to which they have just sworn and whose enforcement can alone protect their lives and property."[13]

A personal animosity developed between Barbé-Marbois and the Directors Reubell and Barras. Barbé-Marbois baited Reubell at a session of the finance committee of the Ancients before the Directory on October 6, 1796, accusing him of making Terrorist appointments.[14] Reubell, on February 24, 1797, charged Barbé-Marbois with sympathy for the Chouans, the Breton rebels, and royalists. Carnot, then a Director, tried to placate his colleague and argued that the former Montagnards and not the Clichiens were the enemies of the Republic.[15] At the Directory's session on May 31, 1797, Carnot tried again to convince Reubell that Barbé-Marbois was a sincere republican and asked him to give up his prejudice against the legislator.[16] Barras, however, suspected Barbè-Marbois of being a member of a royalist committee.[17] The royalists were very active at this time and all who had had a hand in the death of Louis XVI were much alarmed at the prospect of a restoration.

Because of his training in St. Domingue, Barbé-Marbois was particularly active in matters of public finance. His critical, but not too unfriendly, report of November 18, 1796, led to a reduction of two hundred thousand livres in the sum appropriated.[18] He opposed the profits of seigniorage and thought the coinage of money should be at the expense of the state.[19] His observations on the first annual financial report of the Directory were not too severe.[20] He gloried in the freedom of speech which made criticism possible: "Our enemies will be forced to say to themselves, 'that nation is truly free which does not flatter its officials and which is not misled by them'." Barbé-Marbois praised the government, citing the military victories abroad, the return of abundance at home, the discontinuance of paper money without serious disturbances, the return of specie, suppression of disorder, maintenance of the liberty of the press, and the coöperation of the Ancients and the Five Hundred. But one problem remained: "Representatives of the people," he wrote, "if you proceed with the restoration of our finances without being stopped by obstacles unworthy of your courage, you will leave an unperishable monument to our session."

Barbé-Marbois and his circle ardently desired a general European peace, and they urged such a policy on the Directory. He saluted the capture of Trieste as a step toward pacification,[21] and he rejoiced at the Treaty of Campo-Formio with Austria in 1797. "Never has peace been as brilliant, as enduring, as glorious, and as promptly negotiated and concluded as at present."[22]

The elections in the spring of 1797 were an overwhelming victory for the moderates, who had waged a skillful campaign abetted by the royalist press. Of the outgoing third of the Councils, only thirteen former members of the National Convention were reëlected.[23] The Directory was now faced with a hostile majority in the legislature, which tended to break into a right and a center party. The center was strongest in the Ancients where it included Barbé-Marbois, Siméon, Dumas, Portalis, and Thibaudeau.[24] At the first session after the elections, May 21, 1797, Barbé-Marbois was elected president of the Ancients.[25]

The following months marked the height of his influence in the legislature. He was one of the chief sponsors of Barthélemy, an old friend he had first met in Vienna nearly twenty years before, and was largely responsible for his election to the Directory on the retirement of Letourneur.[26] Barthélemy, then popular as the successful negotiator of the treaties of Basel with Prussia and Spain in 1795, was a moderate with royalist leanings. Barbé-Marbois contended at this time, however, that he and his intimates were neither royalist nor republican, but religiously loyal to the constitution and eager to draw a veil over the past by reconciling the divergent factions.[27] "I can say safely," he wrote, "that the royalists would not have found in our society a single individual from whom they were able to hope for support in their designs."[28] In the furtherance of the moderate program a number of laws directed at enemies of the Revolution were repealed. "In the debates relating to these measures nothing occurred that would allow people to say that the new majority was royalist; but there were royalists in that majority, and they were by no means without influence."[29] In July, 1797, Barbé-Marbois joined with a number of other moderates in the Five Hundred and the Ancients in the formation of the moderate Cercle Constitutionnel. The announced purpose of the Cercle was the defense of the constitution against the royalists. Among the members were Pastoret, Boissy d'Anglas, Camille Jordan, and Pichegru in the Five Hundred and Tronçon-Ducoudray, Siméon, Emery, Portalis, Dumas, and Béranger in the Ancients.[30]

During this period Barbé-Marbois was increasingly critical of the Directory's policy. He opposed a proposal to farm out the manufacture of salt, contending that the mines should be under government control.[31] A discussion of St. Domingue afforded him an occasion to urge peace with Great Britain, which he considered essential for real prosperity.[32]

The conduct of foreign affairs aroused his sharpest censure. He declared the department less efficient and more costly than in the days of the *ancien régime*.[33] Even during the Revolution the Committee of Public Safety had conducted a much greater volume of business with a much smaller staff than the present one. Furthermore, Barbé-Marbois felt that the secret bureau of foreign affairs which the Directory maintained constituted a danger to liberty. He called upon the legislature to suppress these kitchen cabinets lest they overshadow the ministries. "Let us keep watch on the maintenance of responsibility, since we are firmly resolved to protect the constitution." He suggested two hundred thousand livres for the secret service rather than the 1,345,000 requested by the department. Of the 350,000 livres to be used as presents to negotiators he could only exclaim: "Good Heavens! 350,000 francs, and since when have republics become five times more liberal than the most luxurious monarchies." Charles Delacroix, the foreign minister, admitted the validity of some of Barbé-Marbois' criticisms and promised that one of his principal aims would be economy.[34]

The election of Barthélemy gave the moderates control of two members of the Directory, for Carnot had sympathized with them for some time. It was he who had arranged the truce between the new third and the Directory after the Babeuf conspiracy. Bitter opposition now developed between Carnot and Barthélemy on the one hand and Barras, La Révellière-Lépeaux, and Reubell on the other. This antagonism was but a reflection of the animosity between the two factions in the legislative councils.

The arrival of the new members in May put the majority of the Directory face to face with a hostile legislature, illustrating the fundamental weakness of the Constitution of 1795. That document provided a system of checks and balances between the legislature and the executive but afforded no way of breaking a deadlock between them. Administrative power, for instance, was vested in the Directory but it had no voice in financial and legislative measures. Solution of the intolerable situation of 1797 lay in the capture of one branch of the Republic by those controlling the other. Barbé-Marbois and the moderates hoped to gain control of the Directory by peaceful and constitutional means.[35] He was thus delighted with the results of the elections in 1797: "Our constitution develops successively its useful and fertile roots and day by day the wisdom and blessing of that fundamental law becomes more evi-

dent."[36] For the Directory the solution of the conflict with
the Councils lay in a *coup d'état,* made easy by the army's
antagonism to the legislature.[37]

Divisions between radicals and moderates,[38] want of
adequate leadership, and lack of tact[39] handicapped the
Councils in their opposition to the executive. Rumor spread
that the Directory planned a resort to force. Carnot ridi-
culed the idea of a plot but urged a more conciliatory attitude on the part of the majority. Many of the deputies
thought the talk of force was merely a means of exerting
pressure in favor of retaining certain revolutionary laws
against the *émigrés* and priests.[40] The group as a whole was
little inclined to concession, but Barbé-Marbois, Portalis,
Siméon, and Tronçon-Ducoudray counseled moderation.

"We were all the more determined to follow this course
since there was no means of resistance. The apathy of the
Parisians, their lack of arms, the memory of Vendémiaire,
the coalition of the armies, the presence of a body of troops
led by Augureau, the reunion of the Terrorists and the
retired officers at Paris, all these circumstances showed the
uselessness of a resort to force."[41]

At first reassured by Carnot's statement, Barbé-Marbois
soon became alarmed again regarding the intentions of
the Directory. On 16 Fructidor [September 2, 1797] he
discussed with his colleagues Lebrun and Villaret-Joyeuse
the possibility of declaring a permanent session of the
Councils or a session in some place other than Paris, but
decided neither procedure offered any advantage.

The Directory moved effectively and secretly. Barbé-Marbois was so poorly informed that on 17 Fructidor he did not realize the proximity of danger. That evening he dined with General Montesquiou and, though friends urged him not to go home, he scoffed at the idea of trouble.[42] At dawn the following day he had a rude awakening by two of his colleagues, Meilland and Gigault-Quisenay, who announced that a cannon shot at 2:30 a. m. had given the signal for an advance on the Tuileries, seat of the legislature. At 4:30, fifteen hundred troops entered the Court of the Tuileries, the guards of the legislature surrendered without a struggle, and soon two thousand more troops arrived. About seven o'clock, members of the two Councils began to assemble, both presidents being present, but the bodies were dissolved by force.[43] Thirty or forty of the Ancients met at Barbé-Marbois' house in the morning. He counseled a firm stand and a return to their legal meeting place, to which they made two unsuccessful trips. Locked out, they decided to resort to the home of Laffon, then the president. Barbé-Marbois made his way unmolested, stopping en route to read the proclamations of the Directory, which charged a royalist plot.[44] Here the assembled group was arrested by an officer who mistook them for members of the Council of Five Hundred meeting in a neighboring house, but he refused to release them, saying "that after what he had taken on himself, a little more or less of compromise was nothing at all."[45] Attended by a horse guard they were sent to prison at 4:00 p. m. and closely guarded that night. Barbé-Marbois was calm, confidently expecting his release the following day.

Yet more than two and one-half years were to elapse before he was to be at liberty again. A rump session of the Councils on the afternoon of 19 Fructidor annulled a number of the elections and ordered the deportation of Directors Barthélemy and Carnot and the prominent opposition deputies, among them Barbé-Marbois. He left Paris without seeing his wife, who was at the family home in Metz. Hearing of the tragedy, she followed the deportees and caught up with them at Blois, where she saw her husband for only fifteen minutes. There occurred a tender farewell in which he commended their daughter, Sophie, and his eighty-year-old mother to the care of his American wife, left alone to fight his battle for freedom.[46] The prisoners, in iron cages, suffered agony on their trip to the coast. Barbé-Marbois wrote that the carriages were without springs and the jolting gave him violent headaches.[47] The party arrived at Rochefort on September 21 and four days later eighteen were shipped to Guiana aboard the *Vaillante*. [48] Thus ended the *coup d'état* of 18 Fructidor, first in a series of unconstitutional attacks which were to culminate in the advent of Bonaparte on 19 Brumaire. Barbé-Marbois' case, like that of the other deputies, was never judged legally, and he made much of this in the journal he kept in Guiana and published unrevised in 1835. No evidence was ever adduced convicting him of royalism, and his own protestations of constitutionalism at this time must stand. Thiers says he was deported only because of his importance in the Ancients.

Although Guiana had enjoyed a sinister reputation since the tragic death of all but a thousand of the twelve thousand colonists Choiseul had sent out in 1763, it was not until the establishment of the penal colony in 1852 that the territory became known as the home of desperate and forlorn criminals. The political exiles of the French Revolution were the first unfortunates to be sent there by the home government. Only the coast was inhabited and even today the interior is a vast unknown wilderness, penetrated only by the fifteen hundred Indians who still remain. In 1797, the population was composed of a handful of Europeans, some mulattoes, a number of Indians, and a majority of negroes. Coöperation of the white colonists and the troops had prevented a slave insurrection and permitted the peaceful application of the Convention's decree freeing the blacks.

Barbé-Marbois' *Journal* is a valuable picture of his life in this wretched country from his arrival at Cayenne, the capital, on November 12, 1797, until his departure on January 21, 1800. Although several of his companions, notably Pichegru, attracted attention on landing, Barbé-Marbois was unnoticed and would have succumbed from the heat had not a kind mulatto voluntarily taken his bags.[49] After a few days at Cayenne the prisoners were transferred some thirty miles up the coast to the pestilential village of Sinnamari, which boasted 110 inhabitants. The trip was made in small open boats. At Sinnamari, Barbé-Marbois took lodgings in the humble home of a Madame Trion, furnishing his bread and wine and paying eight hundred livres a year. The house had a sod floor, but it was comfortable, and its mistress did all she could to make it agreeable. She even made light of his plight to the extent of training a parrot to be taken home to Madame Barbé-Marbois. When the bird was asked "who's there," he responded *"déporté sans jugement."*[50]

Barbé-Marbois settled down at Sinnamari, determined to wait there until he had been pardoned or the Directory had fallen. He passed the time making wooden trinkets and furniture, gardening in early morning and late afternoon, painting, and reading. He studied the Indians and even made an extensive trip to visit a remote tribe in the interior.[51] For six months he received no news. French and American papers were forbidden, but Barbé-Marbois finally got some Dutch ones from the neighboring colony and set to learn the language. "I would have learned Syrian in order to have news,"[52] he wrote. On June 3, 1798, eight of the deportees escaped successfully, but Barbé-Marbois refused to join them, for the flight would make him an *émigré* and render his property subject to confiscation.[53] By September of that year eight of the deportees had died of fever and Barbé-Marbois himself had been ill with it. Of the three men with whom he had been intimate—Tronçon-Ducoudray, Barthélemy, and Laffon—only the last remained in Guiana. Even in France similar interests had drawn the two men together and now they were almost inseparable. They spent five or six hours a day in each other's company, playing checkers about half the time.[54] The military commander found Laffon much the easier of the two to manage, for Barbé-Marbois accepted his status with an injured air and did not go out of his way to cooperate with the officials.[55] Unfortunately for him, the second of the civil governors in this period, Burnell, had a grudge against Barbé-Marbois because the latter's brother had expelled Burnell from Mauritius.[56]

The *Journal* affords evidence of Barbé-Marbois' literary tastes. Quotations from Plato, Virgil, Pliny, Plutarch, Seneca, Ovid, Juvenal, and Tacitus reflect a typical eighteenth-century classical training. More unusual was his knowledge of English literature and the references to Hobbes, Milton, and Hume. Quotations from Thomas Jefferson show the wide reputation already enjoyed by the future American president. Many passages reveal the influence of Rousseau. Such a book lover was not completely without reading matter in his desolate exile, for a number of volumes had been taken from a British vessel captured on the way to Guiana. Barbé-Marbois secured a large share of these books by trading wine for them. With these works and his other interests he whiled away a not too unpleasant existence. In a verse reply[57] to a sympathetic poem from his friends in France he wrote:

> *"Cent fois plutôt mourir ici dans l'innocence*
> *Que de vivre coupable au milieu de Paris."*

Meanwhile the Directory sequestered Barbé-Marbois' property on the charge that he had never been legally removed from the list of *émigrés* in 1793, since the act of the local authorities had not been confirmed in Paris. The government took over his real estate, and his personal property was sold for 8,287 livres 12 sous, of which 6,900 were paid by his wife, who was evidently allowed to buy the property.[58]

Madame Barbé-Marbois came from Metz to Paris to

plead her husband's cause.[59] A copy of the *Philadelphia Advertiser* smuggled into Sinnamari spoke of an interview between her and Fouché in which she was given some hope of Barbé-Marbois' release.[60] On December 26, 1798, she petitioned the Directory to fix a place of exile for him in Europe, and to allow him to live in Cayenne while his case was being considered in Paris.[61] On February 18, 1799, she joined with Mesdames Laffon and Desmolières in a request that their husbands be transferred to the island of Oléron, off the western coast of France,[62] and she repeated the petition on June 7, 1799.[63] Eventually both her requests were granted. Barbé-Marbois left Sinnamari on August 1, 1799, spending the remainder of his exile in Cayenne.

On January 6, 1800, the *Siren* anchored off Cayenne and announced the *coup d'état* of 19 Brumaire and the selection of Bonaparte, Roger-Ducos, and Sieyès as Consuls of the Republic. Sieyès had had a hand in the events of 18 Fructidor and at first Barbé-Marbois and Laffon expected no leniency from the new government. They were surprised, therefore, to find that the new governor of Guiana, Victor Hugues, a former baker who had known Barbé-Marbois in St. Domingue, brought passports for their return to France. The passports were issued on September 2, 1799, before the fall of the Directory, and ordered the prisoners to be taken to Oléron, which held no terrors after Guiana. They went aboard the *Siren* on January 21 and sailed two days later.[64]

One must admire the courage and calm with which Barbé-Marbois endured his twenty-six months in Sinnamari and Cayenne. Fortified by a knowledge of tropical climate gained in St. Domingue, he never gave up hope. He wrote his wife:

"The sun burns me, the rain and wind penetrate my cell, annoying insects torment me during the day and during my sleep. In the midst of so many adversities hope never abandons me a single moment. Eighteen hundred leagues from my native country, my wife and my daughter constantly occupy my thoughts. They are with me at waking; I never lunch without saying to myself that I will not be alone always, and that we should be three. I will see you again; yes, surely, I will see you again."[65]

As the sentiments of the new government were reported pacific, Barbé-Marbois successfully petitioned the Guiana authorities for the privilege of passing Oléron and going directly to France. En route the *Siren* had encounters with two American, and four English, ships, these episodes interestingly illustrating the times. In the Antilles the *Siren* passed an American ship which answered the call of "what news" by saying "a great misfortune, Washington is no more." Barbé-Marbois noted in his *Journal* that Washington had honored him with his friendship and had been very fond of his wife. A few days later they stopped an American boat from Boston, searched her, and found papers authorizing her "to attack the French ships she met and capture them." Although she was a merchant vessel without an ounce of powder, the *Siren* captured and burned her, taking the crew aboard—an incident typical of America's quasi–naval war with France in the administration of President John Adams. Barbé-Marbois, thinking of his American wife and his friends in the United States, keenly regretted the incident. Off Cape Finisterre four English frigates bore down upon the *Siren* and the prisons of Plymouth began to loom before Barbé-Marbois and Laffon. The returning exiles remained on the bridge while the French ship, straining every inch of canvas, ran away in a manner that Barbé-Marbois thought augured well for the future of the French navy. The *Siren* arrived in Brest on February 22, 1800.[66]

A great crowd gathered to welcome the two exiles, surrounding them and offering the news since 19 Brumaire. Barbé-Marbois went straight to Vice-Admiral Bruix, fearing lest he be sent to Oléron as his passport directed. He was overjoyed to find that three weeks before he left Guiana the new government had passed a law ordering that he and Laffon be returned to Paris.[67] The best news of all was the announcement that Bonaparte, Cambacérès, and Lebrun were the new consuls. This seemed too good to be true. "Lebrun, my friend for so many years, the confidant of all my political acts, the sharer of all my thoughts. How I was relieved when his name made me know without question the principles that would inspire the government in the future. Liberty was reborn and will not die with such guardians as Lebrun."[68] Liberty was not reborn, but Barbé-Marbois' political fortunes experienced a remarkable revival.

CHAPTER VII

Minister of the Treasury
Under Napoleon

ON his return from exile Barbé-Marbois found a marked change in public opinion. The attack of 18 Fructidor on constitutional authority had reached its logical conclusion with the destruction of the Directory on 19 Brumaire. Love of liberty was secondary to desire for order and a stable administration. Good government, sound finance, restoration of the church, and peace were the desires of the majority of Frenchmen. By his dedication to this program in 1800 Napoleon made himself master of the country and secured his greatest claim to fame. Bonaparte thought it his mission to heal the wounds of the past and restore the national unity destroyed by the Revolution. To achieve this he drew his servants from all classes and political creeds, Jacobins and royalists sitting down at the same council board. Upon no group did Bonaparte draw more heavily than the former members of the Legislative Councils under the Directory. Both in personnel and policies he inherited more than has been realized from the preceding regime. Barbé-Marbois was to play an honorable and distinguished part in the great reform of the Consulate, particularly in the field of finance.

The First Consul at once showed himself well disposed toward the exile. Bonaparte first received the news of his arrival in France on February 26 while attending a ball at Talleyrand's, and he immediately communicated the good news to Portalis and Dumas, who were present.[1] For his part Barbé-Marbois was struck with admiration for the young warrior. He was apprehensive lest a defeat in the second Italian campaign destroy the First Consul's power in France, and he rejoiced in the great victory of Marengo,[2] expressing contempt for Napoleon's erstwhile enemies who outdid themselves with servile harangues. Soon after his return from Italy, Napoleon invited Barbé-Marbois to visit him at Malmaison, the palace where he and Josephine spent the happiest years of their married life. As they walked through the great park and talked at length the guest felt that the host was judging his ability. He passed the test with flying colors, and on July 24, 1800, was named a member of the Council of State,[3] the body which advised the First Consul and proposed new legislation.

Barbé-Marbois was first employed in the zealous effort to restore the disordered financial and taxation systems of the country. He went as a councilor on mission to the Breton Departments of Ille and Vilaine, Côtes du Nord, Finisterre, and Morbihan,[4] which had been torn by serious civil war over religion and royalism. The restoration of order was so far from complete in this region that Barbé-Marbois found it unwise to assemble the chief officials at Rennes as he had been instructed. Instead he went on circuit himself, *"bien escorté,"* and then met all the prefects of the area at Pontivy. Brigands still operated in the neighborhood, and the prefect of Finisterre was attacked en route and one of his guards killed. Barbé-Marbois blamed the English for much of the disorder. He shrewdly diagnosed the ills and desires of the area: "The inhabitants ask only peace and freedom of worship. They will cherish the government which assures them these blessings."[5] Napoleon soon pacified the region permanently by pursuing this program.

Following his mission in the west, Barbé-Marbois rose rapidly in the esteem of the First Consul. On February 24, 1801, he was appointed director general of the public treasury upon the death of the incumbent of that office. He had charge of disbursements, for which he was accountable to the minister of finance.[6] His administration was so commendable that he received a notable promotion seven months later.

By a decree of September 27, 1801, the Consuls effected a fundamental reorganization in the financial department of the Republic. The office of director general was suppressed and a new ministry of the public treasury created in its stead. Revenues and the income from national property remained as before the province of the minister of finance, but expenditures and the national debt were entrusted to the new ministry.[7] Barbé-Marbois was named to the post and continued to hold this important office for the next five years. Gouverneur Morris read of the appointment in a German gazette and sent his congratulations from America. "I think it highly important, that a man of talents and integrity should occupy that place,"[8] he wrote.

Barbé-Marbois' career throws valuable light on the yet

too little studied financial operations of Napoleon. He saw the First Consul frequently and submitted confidential reports every ten days.[9] The day of his appointment Barbé-Marbois privately recorded his opinion of Napoleon's financial methods. "I find myself," he wrote, "in little accord with the financial principles of a man whose prodigious superiority I recognize every day. He is persuaded that one should spend a great deal, if it is on credit and future chances. Advance, credit, confidence are constantly in his mouth. He seems astonished still to hear contrary maxims from me. . . . I believe he desires absolutely to change my fiscal morality."[10] The minister perforce conformed to Bonaparte's desires but at heart remained so devoted to conservative financial principles that his name became a by-word for frugality. The immediate future, however, made coöperation easy for the First Consul and his minister as the continental peace which ensued for the next two years made it possible to run the state adequately on the ordinary revenues.

The minister often worked at Malmaison, and he left accounts of long evenings spent in council there. The two men were working in the library on October 22, 1801, when Josephine entered, leading Napoleon's younger brother Jerome. Napoleon arose, tapped the lad on the shoulder and said: "You are going to America. Remember the name you bear. Return a man of worth, without having done any of the things that oblige me to send you away." He turned to Barbé-Marbois and added, "Paris, gambling, and the opera were ruining him."[11]

Constant association only increased the minister's

respect for Bonaparte's ability. He wrote in his notes on May 11, 1802: "He is truly admirable in the discussion and examination of business. We work ordinarily *tête à tête* and continually I have occasion to note his capacity for comprehending everything, the quickness and depth of his reflexions. He remembers the least details of conferences already remote."[12]

At this time the treasury was in such a flourishing condition that the minister was able to reduce the discount rate to 1 per cent a month. The bankers were obstinate at first but they came to terms when the business was offered to a new group.[13] Barbé-Marbois presented his accounts for the year X (September 23, 1801–September 22, 1802), as approved by the legislature, with the suggestion that they be published. He wrote with characteristic lack of modesty: "I say without hesitation that this is the first time an account as complete and satisfactory has been prepared."[14]

Napoleon's internal reorganization of France was greatly facilitated by the peace made with England in 1802. Unfortunately neither government considered the Treaty of Amiens more than a truce. Great Britain lost interest in peace when the First Consul refused to negotiate a commercial treaty and she refused to fulfill her treaty obligation to evacuate Malta. Napoleon continued his occupation of Holland and further upset the balance of power on the continent by annexing Swiss and Italian territories. A sharp note crept into Anglo-French relations again in the winter of 1803 and war was resumed in May.[15] Barbé-Marbois viewed the increasing tension with grave misgivings. He felt a war would imperil French interests in general, and he was certain it would undo his achievement at the treasury.

Renewal of war with Great Britain threatened the vast colonial empire which Napoleon had begun to build in the Mississippi Valley and the West Indies. By treaties with Spain, France had secured Santo Domingo in 1795 and Louisiana in 1800. Napoleon had planned to join these with the remnants of the old French Empire, St. Domingue, Martinique, Guadeloupe, and the lesser Indies. He first undertook the reconquest of Haiti where Toussaint L'Ouverture had established a stable negro state which desired self-government under French suzerainty. The failure of the St. Domingue expedition and the hostility of the United States toward French control of New Orleans coincided with the rising hostility of Great Britain. Napoleon suddenly renounced his colonial dream and determined to sell Louisiana to the United States.[16] The operation was entrusted to Barbé-Marbois rather than Talleyrand, then minister of foreign affairs, because of his reputation for honesty and his knowledge of the United States.

The most authoritative French treatment of the cession is the *Histoire de la Louisiane,* which Barbé-Marbois published in 1829.[17] According to that volume, Napoleon summoned the ministers of the treasury and navy and colonies on Easter Sunday, April 10, and asked their advice about selling Louisiana. "I think of ceding it to the United States," he said. "I can hardly say that I cede it to them, for it is not yet in our possession. If I leave the least time to our enemies, I will transmit only an empty title to those Republicans whose friendship I seek. They ask for only one town of Louisiana; but I already consider the Colony as completely lost, and it seems to me that in the hands of that growing power it will be more useful to the policy, and even to the commerce of France than if I should try to keep it."[18] Barbé-Marbois agreed with the First Consul and he was not surprised when Napoleon called him at daybreak the following day, entrusted him with the negotiation, and ordered him to have an interview that very day with Robert R. Livingston, the American minister.[19]

A contemporary note in Barbé-Marbois' memoirs reveals a somewhat different story and indicates either that the *Histoire de la Louisiane* was dressed to suit the temper of its publication date, or that the memory of an old man was faulty. His memoirs report the interview with Napoleon on April 8. Furthermore, Barbé-Marbois records his reply as follows: "Take great care, for we border Mexico with this colony and we ought not to abandon the whole globe to the English." But he offered no further opposition and at once executed Napoleon's command.

Livingston had negotiated unsuccessfully with Talleyrand ever since his own arrival in Paris in 1801, but the foreign minister refused to give him any satisfaction, even denying that France had recovered the colony. At no time, however, had the American government contemplated the acquisition of the vast territory on the west bank of the Mississippi. The interest of the United States in the great river valley was commercial rather than imperial, and its primary object was free navigation to the Gulf of Mexico. When Spain closed the port of New Orleans to American commerce on October 15, 1802, President Jefferson sent Barbé-

Marbois' former acquaintance, James Monroe, to Paris on a special mission to assist Livingston. They were authorized to pay ten million dollars for New Orleans, the island on which it stood, and the Floridas, thought also to be French. In other words, the President intended to purchase only the territory on the east bank of the Mississippi. As a last resort the ministers were instructed to secure the American privilege of depositing goods at New Orleans for re-export. Monroe landed at Havre on April 8, the day Napoleon had his first interview with Barbé-Marbois, but the First Consul's action was in no sense due to Monroe's arrival in France.

Talleyrand surprised Livingston on April 11 by asking what the United States would give for all Louisiana.[20] The American was therefore slightly prepared for an unexpected visit from Barbé-Marbois the following day. Monroe, who had just arrived in Paris, was dining with Livingston when the minister of the treasury was seen walking in the garden. He joined the party for coffee and then explained the purpose of his call to Livingston, whom he invited to a conference any time before eleven that evening.[21] Monroe wanted to accompany his colleague but Livingston objected.[22]

Napoleon had directed Barbé-Marbois to demand fifty million francs for all Louisiana, but the minister, ever keen for a bargain, raised the demand to one hundred million and the cancellation of the American claims for damages inflicted against their shipping since 1800.[23] Because of his residence in America he knew the value placed on the free navigation of the Mississippi. When Livingston expressed surprise at the figure, Barbé-Marbois agreed that it was exorbitant but added that the United States could borrow it. He finally suggested sixty million francs and the settlement of the American claims as a fair price, and offered to propose this to Napoleon as a basis of negotiation.

The remainder of April was consumed in dickering over the price. Both parties were anxious to conclude the business and it was simply a question of which one would first accede to the demands of the other. On April 15, the American ministers offered forty million.[24] Barbé-Marbois feigned indifference and said he no longer considered the matter in his hands. He held out no hope of an arrangement below sixty million, hinting that Napoleon might change his mind about selling at all. By April 21, Barbé-Marbois could write Talleyrand that the negotiation was *"en bon chemin."*[25] Livingston and Monroe had already agreed to his proposal. Napoleon drew up a projected treaty and set the price again at one hundred million.[26] Barbé-Marbois dropped it to eighty million on April 27, with the understanding that twenty million was to be devoted to satisfying the claims of American citizens against France. Two days later Livingston and Monroe accepted these terms. The treaty and two conventions which comprised the transaction were all dated April 30, though the negotiations were actually completed a week later.

Rarely has a cession of such magnitude been accompanied by so much good will on the part of all concerned. Barbé-Marbois' American sympathies, his knowledge of the Mississippi question, and his acquaintance with the American ministers made him an ideal negotiator. He himself spoke to Napoleon of "the good faith" that had attended the discussions.[27] Monroe wrote Barbé-Marbois: "In society with my respectable colleague, to have met an old friend on the occasion, who had experienc'd as well as myself some vicissitudes in the extry. movements of the epoch, in wch. we live is an incident wch. adds not a little to the gratification which I derive from the event."[28] James Madison, Secretary of State, found pleasure in an event which awoke "recollections both of a public & private nature so agreeable" to both him and Barbé-Marbois. He must have smiled at the thought that the young French diplomat who supported Spain's position on the Mississippi during the American Revolution should have been the instrument for the destruction of her power in the great valley.

The cession of Louisiana was one of the most important events in modern history. One could make a good case for the thesis that it was one of the most significant acts of Napoleon's career. Livingston, Monroe, and Barbé-Marbois all realized at the time that they were principals in a great drama, and in subsequent years made much of their parts in the transaction. The Frenchman caught more than a glimpse of the future of the great territory, for in 1829 he prophesied a population of one hundred million for the United States by the end of the century. He associated himself so thoroughly with the cession that this is the episode by which he is best remembered today.

As minister of the treasury, Barbé-Marbois also handled the financial arrangements of the Louisiana Purchase. Despite the war, the English houses of Hope and Baring

"*The Transfer of Louisiana to the United States*"

Painting by T. de Thulstrup

Barbé-Marbois During the Restoration

Portrait by Maurin

agreed to buy the bonds created by the American government. On July 25, after the outbreak of hostilities, Alexander Baring conferred in Paris with Barbé-Marbois[29] and soon sailed for the United States to bring the bonds back personally to England.

Bonaparte was so delighted at the success of the negotiation with the American ministers that he made Barbé-Marbois a gift of 192,000 francs.[30] The money arrived at a very convenient time, as the minister, for the first time in his life, was experiencing financial difficulty.[31] This embarrassment arose from the necessity of providing a suitable dowry for his daughter, Sophie, who in 1804 was married to Charles-François-Paul Lebrun, the son of Barbé-Marbois' dear friend and political confidant. The match was a suitable one and united two families long bound by similar interests. Young Lebrun proved a devoted son and a lifelong friend of his father-in-law.

In the summer of 1803, Barbé-Marbois' work at the treasury increased with the demands of the war. He traveled to Belgium where he reported great admiration for Napoleon and staunch attachment to France.[32] The good interests of the department forced him to replace its agents in Hanover, where there was both inefficiency and corruption. Funds ran low and in some areas the pay of the soldiers was in arrears.[33] False rumors circulated on the Bourse and the operations of the treasury became more difficult. All the while more and more money was required for the army at Boulogne, which was preparing to invade England.

Napoleon never made adequate financial preparation for his wars. He refused to levy unusual taxes or to float heavy loans and proceeded on the revolutionary theory that the conquered enemy should feed his troops and pay the cost of the conflict. The inevitable result was a series of difficulties for the treasury. As Barbé-Marbois wrote, Napoleon "created embarrassments that appeared insurmountable and when the crises came he invented expedients which nearly always succeeded, but generally at the price of justice and sincerity, and often of the future."[34] The fundamentally divergent opinions of the two men led to increased friction. On August 17 occurred one of those flashes of temper for which Napoleon was noted. He tossed a paper across the table at Malmaison to Barbé-Marbois with the curt remark that he was astounded to receive such a report. The minister says in his memoirs that he offered to resign, but his later sycophancy makes this doubtful.

Minor irritations, however, did not blind Barbé-Marbois to the greatness of the Corsican. "If I compare him to other princes who have governed and who govern in Europe," he wrote, "what a difference between them and this great genius. There has never been, I think, a case of so great an ability united to a blindness which leads him to sacrifice everything for his own glory. He is good, human, worthy of governing a great people. If experience moderates his impetuosity, France will never have been governed by so great a man."[35]

Barbé-Marbois' memoirs of this period are filled with intimate glimpses of the Bonaparte family. There were dinners at Malmaison and *têtes-à-têtes* with Josephine, already disturbed by rumors of her husband's desire for a divorce. The news of Jerome's marriage in Baltimore to

Elizabeth Patterson sent Napoleon into a rage. He stormed in front of Barbé-Marbois, spoke of a special law for marriage in his family, and called the father of the bride a worthless fellow who had arranged the match. For some unaccountable reason Barbé-Marbois, rather than the minister of the navy, sent a frigate to bring Jerome back to France. The minister complained that the United States might well have given the youth passage on one of their own naval vessels.[36]

In the winter of 1803–1804, a group of royalists led by Georges Cadoudal, the Vendéan, and Pichegru planned an attempt on the life of the First Consul. The police arrested the principals in short order, and it was at this time that the Bourbon Duc d'Enghien was executed on a false charge of conspiring against Bonaparte. Josephine poured out her sorrow over the execution to the minister of the treasury and said her husband had shed innocent blood for the first time.[37] Barbé-Marbois was much disturbed by a rumor that he had had an interview with Pichegru, who had been deported with him to Guiana after 18 Fructidor. It was also reported that Barbé-Marbois' name, along with those of Siméon and Portalis, was on a list found at Ettenheim, comprising the persons on whom the Duc d'Enghien could rely.[38]

Barbé-Marbois wrote at once to Napoleon, denouncing the baseless rumors and assuring him of his allegiance. He asserted that he had not seen Pichegru nor had he had any relations with him since Pichegru left Guiana six years before.[39] Napoleon had not heard of the rumors and he dismissed them without further thought. He knew that Barbé-

Marbois owed too much to his regime to engage in royalist intrigue.

Barbé-Marbois inwardly doubted the wisdom of making Napoleon Emperor, but he voiced no opposition when the question was raised in the spring of 1804. He admitted, with a touch of shame, that he was silenced by Bonaparte's favor and the general acquiescence of the nation to the proposed change. His disgust at the titles of the new court officials was communicated only to his memoirs. As he saw it, the coronation ceremony on December 2 aroused little enthusiasm or affection for the Emperor; Napoleon acted like a school boy in stage clothes.[40]

Barbé-Marbois' own personal prosperity reflects the great national recovery under the consulate. After his return from Guiana he did not take up his residence again at Metz, but in partnership with his daughter on April 21, 1804, purchased the chateau of Noyers in Normandy from the Count of Lenoncourt for the price of 273,500 francs. This was the first, and most considerable, of twenty purchases of real estate which Barbé-Marbois made in the department of Eure within the next nine years. By 1813, his total investments were nearly 650,000 francs and he was lord of a vast domain.[41] He also retained his property in Metz and at Buchy, which had been restored to him on his return from exile.

The remainder of his life was to be associated with this fertile Norman country rather than his native Lorraine. The merchant's son played the paternalistic role of a noble of the *ancien régime*. The chateau at Noyers was a fit setting for such a life. It had been designed by Mansart in the age

of Louis XIV, and its fountains and gardens were minia-
ture reproductions of those that adorned Versailles. One
has only to compare it with the simple Louis XV house at
Buchy to see how much its master had prospered in less
than a decade.

Naturally one seeks the explanation of this extraordinary financial success. It could not be speculation at the
treasury, for Napoleon kept a vigilant eye on his ministers;
furthermore, Barbé-Marbois was considered the soul of
honesty by his contemporaries. The records of the department of Eure in 1804 give a complete picture of his personal fortune. The annual income from his land at Buchy
was 9,600 francs, and the house at Metz brought in eighteen
hundred more. His own share of the revenue at Noyers was
six thousand francs. *Rentes* accounted for another one thousand francs, making a total income of 18,400 francs a year
from property. His salary as minister was eighty thousand
francs.[42] He thus earned nearly $20,000 a year, a very con-
siderable income for those days. When one remembers that
Barbé-Marbois was a good business man and also very
close fisted, it is easy to see how he secured the funds to
invest heavily in Norman real estate.

In August, 1804, Barbé-Marbois made his first prominent appearance in the public life of his newly adopted
department. Napoleon appointed him president of the electoral college for the nomination of two candidates to the
Senate. The election was held at Évreux, the department
capital. Évreux is one of the charming small cities of provincial France. A tiny stream, the Iton, wanders quietly
through the town and is traversed by several hundred

bridges. Nearly all of the city's public buildings today were formerly the property of the church, and there are many other links with the *ancien régime*. The great Gothic-Renaissance cathedral and its environs have hardly changed since Barbé-Marbois walked in their shadow over a century ago.

The departmental records and the minister's correspondence provide an interesting account of how elections to the Senate of the Empire were conducted. Barbé-Marbois sent an imperial decree to Masson de St. Amand, the prefect, on July 21, informing him that the election had been set for August 8. He thanked the prefect for his proffered hospitality but asked instead that "a simple and comfortable" lodging be prepared for him and his secretary.[43] A general letter to all the electors was distributed, convoking the college and announcing that it would last seven days, unless the business were finished sooner.

Barbé-Marbois' arrival in Évreux was greeted with a salute of fifteen cannon. At 10:00 A. M. of the appointed day the college opened its session in the cathedral under his presidency. After mass the president read the official papers authorizing the election and then "with emotion" delivered a speech "which left a profound impression in the heart of all the electors." He deplored the excesses of the Revolution and lauded Napoleon to the skies. "Of our long and painful Revolution," he declared, "there remain only the advantages which the French people desired when it asked, not the overthrow of the established order, but beneficial reforms and institutions adjusted to the progress, enlightenment, and needs of a greater civilization." The prefect was then chosen secretary and, after two ballots, a couple of talesmen were named. So ended the first day.[44]

The following morning Barbé-Marbois received 135 out of the 150 votes cast on the first ballot and was immediately declared elected. No other candidate received more than twenty-seven votes on this ballot, but on the third ballot another got seventy-six votes and thus became the second nominee.[45] The college ended its session with a grand banquet on the evening of the tenth, and Barbé-Marbois returned to Paris the next day. For his part it had been an extremely pleasant and flattering experience.

Barbé-Marbois wrote Napoleon that his own election was motivated by a desire to please the Emperor and fulfill his wishes. Everywhere he had seen striking testimonials of affection for His Majesty.[46] Despite this flattery, Barbé-Marbois did not secure a seat in the Senate. The electoral college only nominated the candidates. The final choice lay with Napoleon and for some reason he failed to select Barbé-Marbois at this time.

Barbé-Marbois was much disturbed by the condition of the treasury in 1804 and he suggested some radical changes to Napoleon. "I plead with Your Majesty," he wrote, "by the sincerest attachment to my country and to your person, Sire, to undertake today an indispensable reform."[47] Nothing was done, but Barbé-Marbois seemed reassured a few days later when he returned from a visit to the army at Boulogne.

The year XIII (September 23, 1804–September 22, 1805) began in an extremely quiet and satisfactory manner for the treasury. *Rentes* were paid punctually, and the various government bureaus received their appropriations promptly. On December 8, the minister wrote Napoleon that the work of his department proceeded smoothly and there was nothing particular to report. This happy situation continued for the first six months of the year, and at no time since the inauguration of the Consulate had treasury obligations been so sought after by bankers and investors. The minister's chief annoyances were his colleagues, who protested against the reduction in salaries which had been ordered for the year XIII. Talleyrand, the avaricious minister of foreign affairs, and Berthier, the minister of war, were so insistent that Barbé-Marbois was forced to present their complaints to Napoleon.[48] As late as May 6, 1805, the minister could write that the work of the treasury proceeded "with great facility."[49]

Barbé-Marbois retained all the zeal for efficiency and all the hatred of corruption that had marked his intendancy in St. Domingue. He set high standards for himself and he expected them in others. Officials who failed to conform were reported to the Emperor, and, in the case of minor employees, summarily dismissed. On February 16, 1805, one finds him reporting the receiver general of Loire Inférieure for disorder and general inefficiency in his office.[50] An inspection showed the receiver general for Yonne to be four hundred thousand francs in arrears. He had lent government funds to an acquaintance, who had subsequently been forced into bankruptcy, and had himself speculated unsuccessfully in the wine market. Barbé-Marbois was lenient enough in this case to propose the removal of the receiver general for his "complete incapacity" rather than for his dishonesty.[51] As a private citizen he urged the reorganization of his own department of Eure, where there was great need of an energetic prefect who could make his authority respected.[52]

At no time in his ministry did Barbé-Marbois treat such far-flung interests as in the late spring and summer of 1805. Much of his correspondence is concerned with naval questions. These were the months before Trafalgar, when Napoleon still hoped to use his navy for a successful descent on England. Barbé-Marbois reported on movements of the French fleet in the West Indies, the operations of Nelson in the Mediterranean, and the talk of a *levée en masse* in Great Britain to repel the French.[53] He read the English newspapers assiduously and often communicated their contents to the Emperor. The rapid increase in the territory and interests of the Empire added to the work of the treasury. On June 19, Barbé-Marbois asked Napoleon whether the Ligurian Republic, formerly Genoa, had been annexed to France and if so what provisions the Emperor cared to make for its financial service.[54] Somewhat characteristically Napoleon had failed to inform his minister of the change in the map of Italy. At this time Barbé-Marbois warmly seconded Napoleon's plans to close the Portuguese ports to British shipping.[55] He urged support for the West Indies and asked that the islands not be abandoned to their own resources during the war.

In the summer of 1805 the minister had a pleasant reminder of his residence and services in Bavaria a generation before. The Elector of that country, a steadfast ally of Napoleon, decorated the former French chargé d'affaires at Munich with the Order of St. Hubert. Barbé-Marbois utilized the occasion to attest anew his devotion to the Emperor. "The motto and statutes of the order," he wrote, "impose upon the one who receives it a constant fidelity to the one who gives it. An even more powerful law makes it a duty and a pleasure for me to retain this sentiment toward Your Majesty all my life."[56] At the moment this extravagant language was no doubt sincere, for up to this time Barbé-Marbois' tenure of office had been pleasant. As long as France was at war with England alone he could meet the demands of the government, though Napoleon's unorthodox methods worried him a great deal. The task became immeasurably more difficult in July, when Pitt formed the Third Coalition and Russia and Austria were added to France's enemies. The strain of continental war soon produced the crisis Barbé-Marbois feared.

CHAPTER VIII

A Financial Crisis that Threatened
the Empire

FRANCE'S war against Austria and Russia greatly complicated the problems of the treasury and the last six months
of 1805 were very unhappy ones for Barbé-Marbois. The
Emperor's growing criticism of his administration dis-
tressed him and as early as August he spoke of resigning.
"When Your Majesty judges me ready for retirement," he
wrote, "I will go quietly and I will conduct myself in a
manner to merit your esteem."[1]

The treasury became dependent upon the bankers and
the army contractors. The discounting of treasury obligations and the paper of the receivers general, who collected
the taxes, had been entrusted for the year XIII (September
22, 1804–September 21, 1805) to an organization known as
the *Négociants Réunis*. This company also furnished food
supplies for the army. In 1804, it had assumed the further
burden of financing the subsidy which the Spanish government owed Napoleon as the price of its failure to declare
war on England. Desprez, who was also regent of the Bank
of France, represented the company in its relations with
the treasury; Vanlerberghe headed the vast organization

that fed the army; while Ouvrard, as head of the company, took charge of the gigantic operations in Spain.[2]

Ouvrard was one of the great speculators of modern times. Barbé-Marbois later described him to Napoleon as "a bold man, engaging without sufficient foresight in the most dangerous enterprises, fertile in resources for getting out of them, cool in danger, capable of organizing, undertaking, and conducting very large operations to a certain point, but exposing himself to too many changes and lacking personally the sense of safety and love of order without which one should not approach the treasury."[3] This man went to Spain with the blessing of the Emperor in September, 1804, and there undertook a vast extension of his relations with the Spanish government. He agreed to supply wheat to supplement the scanty Spanish crop which had caused a famine in parts of the peninsula. He took over the financing of the *Casa de consolidación,* which sustained the obligations of the Spanish government and also controlled the tobacco monopoly and the operation of the mercury mines. Funds were advanced to the *Casa* against bonds that were to be paid from the sale of confiscated church property in Spain, a highly uncertain operation. The supreme achievement of this French financial genius was the acquisition of a monopoly of the trade with the Spanish colonies for the duration of the war, which Spain had entered on December 14, 1804, and the privilege of importing piastres from Mexico, paying three francs seventy-five centimes for coins which had a par value of five francs. It was planned to bring them to Europe in neutral vessels, preferably American, and market them in Amsterdam. Ouvrard secured the coöperation of Labouchère, head of the Amsterdam office of the London firm of Hope. Since England was in sore need of precious metals, Pitt agreed to allow shipments from Amsterdam to London. The project was a highly complex one and could hardly be put in operation before 1806.[4] In the meantime, the *Négociants Réunis* were to encounter difficulties which their master mind had not envisaged.

Barbé-Marbois feared that the multiple and gigantic enterprises of Ouvrard might compromise the credit of the *Négociants Réunis,* and he proposed that the discounting of treasury obligations and the paper of the receivers general be given to another group of bankers for the year XIV (September 22, 1805–September 21, 1806). He planned to keep Desprez, in whom he had great confidence, but also suggested Perrégaux, Récamier, and Doyen, who had not been connected with the company. Napoleon opposed the change in such a difficult period and the old bankers were retained. Thus the responsibility for entrusting so much business to Ouvrard and his associates in the year XIV rests directly with the Emperor himself.[5]

A mild crisis occurred in Paris in August. There was a great scarcity of specie due to the shipment of large quantities to Boulogne, Brest, and Italy for the army and to the export of precious metals in return for colonial products. A run on the Bank of France occurred, and Barbé-Marbois had to deplete the provinces to stop the panic.[6]

Vanlerberghe appealed to Barbé-Marbois for assistance in this crisis and the minister, considering his services essential to the army, made him an advance in the form of bonds of the receivers general.[7] Barbé-Marbois was led to do this by the assurance of his own secretary, Roger, that Vanlerberghe's accounts were solvent. Roger is reputed to have received one million francs for his duplicity. The turning over of these bonds was Barbé-Marbois' primary mistake in his relations with the *Négociants Réunis*. He acted without authority and without informing the Emperor or the other ministers. It was this action for which Napoleon blamed him most.

Ouvrard lacked the funds to pay for the wheat and naval stores he had promised Spain, and he appealed to Vanlerberghe. In September, 1805, the latter had received the regular appropriation for army supplies for the next three months and he now used part of this to support his colleague, expecting that Ouvrard could reimburse him before the funds would be needed to satisfy his own creditors. But Ouvrard's difficulties were not so easily resolved. The steady shipment of specie from Spain to France, without the receipt of the usual quantities from America, depleted the peninsula and produced a first class crisis in September. The notes of the *Casa de consolidación* fell 58 per cent, ruining the creditors of the state, the most important of these being Ouvrard. He could send no further piastres to France, so, as Napoleon said, France instead of receiving a subsidy had actually paid one to Spain.

The critical situation which ensued in the Empire concerned primarily the Bank of France and Vanlerberghe. Because of Desprez's dual position, the Bank had been very liberal in rediscounting the government obligations held by the *Négociants Réunis* and had also accorded an advance upon the piastres expected from Spain. The inflation produced by the issuance of these bank notes was especially serious, since the government was not in position to redeem the bonds of the receivers general held by the Bank. This arose because Barbé-Marbois, in his efforts to sustain the *Négociants Réunis,* had allowed Desprez to take all the cash in the coffers of the receivers general. In return Desprez had given his own notes, rather grandly called "the bonds of Monsieur Desprez." When the Bank later presented the bonds of the receivers general it found nothing but Desprez's promissory notes in the treasury.

Vanlerberghe was forced to confess to Barbé-Marbois that the supply service of the army was endangered by the losses of Ouvrard, but he did not disclose the illegal use he had made of French funds. Vanlerberghe admitted a deficit of fifty-nine million francs on October 5 and, on October 13, told Barbé-Marbois he would fail unless supported by the treasury.[8] The minister had the highest confidence in the contractor and great personal sympathy for his embarrassment. He appealed to the Spanish government and received some assistance for Ouvrard's creditors and for Vanlerberghe, the latter in the form of a ten million florin loan to Spain in Amsterdam. These efforts of Godoy, the Spanish prime minister, led Barbé-Marbois to hope that the crisis would be passed safely. He thought all would be well if the treasury could only get by October.[9]

Barbé-Marbois felt support of Vanlerberghe was necessary at all costs. His failure would involve contractors throughout the country and would produce a major financial crisis at a critical stage of the campaign against Austria. As he explained to General Beurnonville, the French ambassador in Madrid, the Coalition had a concerted program to produce bankruptcy in France by denuding the country of precious metals. Its plan had been aided by the loss of France's colonies, which forced her to export specie in return for such colonial products as coffee, cocoa, and sugar.[10] This was a correct version of the Coalition's policy. France's enemies had high hopes of a crisis within the country. Some expected an uprising against the Emperor; this explains General Mack's foolhardy dash toward France and his consequent defeat and capture by Napoleon at Ulm on October 22. More cautious adversaries of the Emperor thought a financial crash at home would thwart his military operations against Austria and Russia.

September and October were terrible months for the worried minister of the treasury. On September 25 he sent the Emperor this disquieting news: "We have used all our available resources. We have no margin on any side, and our operations are carried out with extreme difficulty. The service [of the treasury] could be stopped by a single untoward event."[11] Specie simply could not be procured at Lyons and in the south. Operations on Milan were so difficult that Barbé-Marbois had little hope for the organization of any regular service for Italy.[12]

The measures of the autumn merely delayed the inevitable crisis. The supply of specie from Spain ceased completely, the Bank's notes were thus inadequately covered, and the treasury was without funds to redeem the bonds of the receivers general which the *Négociants Réunis* had discounted at the Bank. Barbé-Marbois' worst fears were now realized. He felt unable to bear the burden alone any longer and he asked that Mollien, director of the sinking fund, be permitted to deliberate with him and Gaudin, the minister of finance. He thought of retiring and humbly admitted that one better acquainted with the business of the Bank and matters of foreign exchange would be more qualified to fill his office in such troubled times.[13]

The public unrest led Joseph Bonaparte to call a conference of the minister of finance, Barbé-Marbois, Fouché, who was the minister of police, and Louis Bonaparte. It was decided to support Vanlerberghe, for his bankruptcy would have been disastrous. He had seven or eight hundred agents all over France and ten thousand creditors. After some difficulty, Barbé-Marbois induced the Bank to make new advances to him.[14]

A panic seized the holders of bank notes and a run ensued. All funds left with the receivers general and all the available resources of the neighboring departments were called to Paris. The Bank was allowed to convert only five to six hundred thousand francs a day. Tellers counted the money slowly in order to gain time. Fouché set up a system of numbers to be distributed in the *arrondissements* by the mayors, who knew the legitimate needs of their fellow citizens.[15] Barbé-Marbois issued a decree, assuring the public that "the notes of the Bank could not in any sense suffer a single centime of loss!"[16] After a few days the demands on the Bank returned to normal.

A second conference, attended by Joseph Bonaparte, Louis Bonaparte, and the ministers of war, the navy, finance, interior, and the public treasury, decided that Vanlerberghe should be assisted further from the treasury.

Here the princes and other ministers learned for the first time of the steps Barbé-Marbois had already taken to support Vanlerberghe. Vanlerberghe appeared and testified that the plight of the company was due to conditions in Spain. He requested twenty million francs, but Barbé-Marbois thought ten million would tide him over the next two weeks. By that time the decision of Napoleon could be received from Austria.[17] The minister was gambling always on a victory at the front, which would alleviate the political and financial condition at home.

Unfortunately, a number of bankruptcies now occurred, the most significant being that of the great banker Récamier, whom Barbé-Marbois had proposed as one of the treasury bankers for the year XIV. The loss involved in this failure alone amounted to twelve million francs. Barbé-Marbois spent a great deal of time receiving and encouraging people who were menaced by bankruptcy, very conscientiously seeing all who cared to call on him.[18] The bankruptcies caused the bank notes to fall, and it was more obvious than ever that Vanlerberghe must be supported at all costs. The future depended on Napoleon's orders and the measures taken by the ministry of war and the navy for servicing their departments.[19]

Barbé-Marbois was like a drowning man clutching at a straw. Letters from his own special emissary in Spain were reassuring, and the minister began to hope that Ouvrard would succeed with his plans after all. But further aid from the treasury would be necessary for some time and he pled with Napoleon to view the matter in its entirety and not think harshly of him. Barbé-Marbois was convinced that "no minister had ever found himself in such a difficult position."[20] The news that Napoleon had entered Vienna made him feel his sacrifices had been worth-while. The one thing he thought necessary was the Emperor's presence in Paris. He implored him to return as soon as possible; every day gained would be of the greatest value.[21] If the Emperor could not return immediately, the minister felt it would have a stabilizing effect if only the date of his expected arrival could be announced.[22]

Vanlerberghe needed ten millions more in order to meet his obligations and save his creditors from bankruptcy.[23] Napoleon eased the strain at Paris by dispensing with further shipment of funds to Italy and to the Grand Army. This was the first communication Barbé-Marbois had received from the Emperor in two months.[24] The pleasure of news from Napoleon was destroyed, however, by a letter of November 22 disapproving of the minister's action in advancing funds to Vanlerberghe. The Emperor also criticized the Bank severely.[25]

This very discouraging letter from his master found the sixty-year-old minister working day and night verifying figures and trying to find some way out of the prolonged difficulty. Desprez, to whom he had transferred the privilege of discounting government obligations, did not have sufficient resources to continue the service.[26] More and more Barbé-Marbois desired the presence of Napoleon in Paris.[27] This seemed the only way to restore confidence in financial circles, for Récamier's failure had been followed by eighteen failures, eight of them at Marseilles.[28] However, by December 23, the minister felt the crisis had passed. Bank notes returned to par. Specie was abundant in Paris, since funds had been called in from the provinces.[29] Barbé-Marbois felt the affairs of the *Négociants Réunis* would be terminated as happily as circumstances permitted.

These hopeful and self-excusing letters found no favor with the implacable Emperor. Barbé-Marbois' conduct had irritated him on a number of occasions in the summer and autumn, and he was in a severe mood when the crisis occurred. He wrote from Schönbrunn on December 15 that Barbé-Marbois had given four years of good service because he had followed Napoleon's advice; now for four months he had not followed it and matters were critical. The Emperor quite unjustly claimed he had foreseen what would occur. "You are a very honest man," he wrote, "but I can only believe that you are surrounded by rogues."[30] Barbé-Marbois, in reply, repeated the reasons that had led him to support the *Négociants*. He admitted that his letters had been too frequent and at times ill-advised.[31]

With the passing of the crisis the minister of the treasury recovered his accustomed self-assurance. By January 6, he was so composed that he began in his own mind to assume the role of a hero. He wrote Joseph Bonaparte that he had never merited the Emperor's confidence so much as in his handling of the affair with Vanlerberghe.[32] At this time Talleyrand congratulated Barbé-Marbois on the successful conclusion of the crisis with the company and at the Bank.[33] The news of Napoleon's impending return had a stabilizing effect on the Bourse.[34]

The Emperor returned to France after one of the greatest triumphs of his career. The defeat of the Austrian and

Russian forces at Austerlitz, on December 2, had been a superb military achievement. Its political consequences were no less brilliant, as Austria was forced to sue for peace. It angered the returning Caesar that at the very moment of his success in battle his position had been threatened by a financial tangle at home. As he hurried across South Germany his indignation mounted against the minister whom he held responsible for the near-fiasco. From Karlsruhe, on January 21, he dispatched a burning letter to Barbé-Marbois, reminding him that nothing should have been paid out of the treasury without the authorization of the Emperor and the ministers of the respective departments.[35] Napoleon wrote Joseph: "I send you an unsealed letter for the minister of the public treasury. You will read it and forward it to him, after sealing it. I do not yet know whether this is folly or treason, but the Coalition has no more useful ally than my minister. I suspend my judgment until on my arrival, which is near at hand, I can myself verify the facts and discover the truth. As a matter of fact, I believe the man has betrayed me. Meanwhile do not alarm him. Tell him there is but one way of dispersing the storm which is about to burst over him: it is to restore the bonds which have been taken from the treasury."[36]

Napoleon arrived in Paris on the evening of January 26 and the following day held a council meeting which lasted from 8:00 A. M. to 5:00 P. M. Present were Gaudin, Barbé-Marbois, Mollien, his first assistant, Ouvrard, Vanlerberghe, Desprez, and Roger, the treasury official who had misinformed Barbé-Marbois about the state of the *Négociants Réunis*. "M. Barbé-Marbois began [his] report with all the calm of one whose conscience does not reproach him for a thing," wrote Mollien.[37] Napoleon refused to listen and demanded that Ouvrard, Vanlerberghe, and Desprez give all their possessions to the state. The dictator simply confiscated their property without bothering with legalities.[37] Napoleon's truly terrible temper was at its worst that day.

In the evening the Emperor, slightly calmed, decided to dismiss Barbé-Marbois and to replace him with Mollien, who held the position until the fall of the Empire. The minister of the interior was ordered to convey the news to the two men. Barbé-Marbois was told that the change was motivated by "considerations relative to the good of my service."[38] The Emperor quite unfairly wrote that the minister had committed "only follies" during his absence.[39] On his dismissal Barbé-Marbois is reputed to have cried: "I dare hope Your Majesty will not accuse me of being a thief." "I would have a hundred times preferred it," replied the Emperor, "knavery has limits, stupidity none at all."[40] This story may or may not be true. In acknowledging his dismissal, Barbé-Marbois did write Napoleon a dignified letter: "In retirement, Sir, I shall hold dear the memory of the favors with which you honored me during six years, and the sorrow I experience in losing your confidence is diminished by the certainty that nothing can deprive me of the esteem of Your Majesty. I am, with the profoundest [respect] for Your Majesty, the very faithful and very submissive subject, Barbé-Marbois."[41]

It would be quite unjust to hold Barbé-Marbois primarily responsible for the crisis of 1805. Napoleon must be blamed severely for beginning the conflict without sufficient financial reserves. It was his anticipation of subsidies from Spain that opened the grand field of speculation in that country to Ouvrard. Barbé-Marbois' mistake lay in entrusting funds in the treasury and the coffers of the receivers general to Vanlerberghe without adequate security and without the authorization of the Emperor. He was misinformed regarding the affairs of the *Négociants Réunis* by his secretary. When he learned the truth, the minister felt it imperative to save the vast interests throughout France dependent upon Vanlerberghe. The success of this operation should have moderated Napoleon's rage at the deficit of more than 140,000,000 francs which he found on his return. The Emperor's stern measures recovered most of this sum,[42] thus showing that Barbé-Marbois had not erred seriously in his estimates of the company's assets.

Had Napoleon been in a forgiving mood he might easily have retained Barbé-Marbois in office. The minister had made a serious mistake of judgment, but there were mitigating circumstances. Mollien sympathized with him and voiced no criticism of his former superior in his memoirs. Earlier irritation with the minister no doubt influenced Napoleon in the heat of the council session. The fundamentally different fiscal philosophies of the two men had produced a number of annoying incidents during the war. It provoked Napoleon that such a notorious stickler for the law should himself step beyond his authority. Ironically enough, the minister fell because of an infraction which he would not himself have pardoned in a subordinate.

Barbé-Marbois now considered his public career ended

and he retired to the quiet of Noyers. For the next twenty months the sixty-year-old statesman devoted himself to his estate, purchased more land, and indulged his deep passion for agriculture. His Norman friend, Antoine Passy, relates an interesting story about Barbé-Marbois at this time.[43] The former minister brought a box of gold from Paris, reputed to contain one hundred thousand francs, and in good early-nineteenth-century style buried it in the grounds of the chateau. A few days later he observed that someone had been near the hiding place, and excavation that night revealed that the treasure had been stolen. A few days passed without any trace of the money. Then one Sunday a *gendarme* who had been apprised of the theft saw the son of Barbé-Marbois' gardener spend a gold piece at a country fair. The gardener confessed to the crime on promise of pardon and all but a few hundred francs were recovered.

Napoleon was not vindictive and once his anger cooled he felt kindly disposed toward his former servant. Barbé-Marbois was suddenly called from his agrarian retreat back to office in Paris in 1807. On September 28, the Emperor made him first president of the newly created Cour des Comptes.[44] This institution, which audited the accounts of the Empire, was one of the great administrative achievements of Napoleon.[45]

Barbé-Marbois probably owed this mark of the Emperor's favor to the intercession of his friend Lebrun, now Archtreasurer of the Empire. Lebrun's duties involved assisting the ministers of finance and the public treasury in the preparation of accounts and in the presentation of estimates for the annual budget. By reason of his position he was entrusted with the actual organization of the Cour des Comptes. He thus had the privilege of presiding at the formal installation of his friend as first president.

The occasion was a gala one. A procession of seven carriages escorted by a detachment of cavalry proceeded to the Augustinian monastery where the Cour des Comptes was to hold its sessions until 1842.[46] Lebrun, in a happy frame of mind, paid high tribute to the president: "[The Emperor] recognized in you deep feeling beneath an austere exterior, an absolute devotion to his glory, an inviolable fidelity to your duty . . . and suddenly without your daring to ask a favor, without friendship even pronouncing your name . . . His Majesty recalls you to functions linked with the greatest interests of the Empire."[47] If this be true, Napoleon was at least aware that the appointment would be pleasing to the high financial figures of the government. Mollien rejoiced at the appointment. His laudatory comment shows that he had not lost respect for his former chief because of the *Négociants Réunis* affair: "Scarcely had he begun to exercise his functions [at the Cour des Comptes] when he was surrounded with the respect and confidence which had been the fruit of centuries for the ancient magistrature."[48]

This was one of the best appointments Napoleon ever made, and Barbé-Marbois filled the position continuously until 1834, except for the Hundred Days. The first president was eminently fitted and devoted to the detailed drudgery which the office required. In good weather Barbé-Marbois always walked from his apartment (87 Rue de Grenelle) to the Cour. He was so regular in his arrival at the office that the merchants around the Pont Neuf used to remark on seeing him: "It's nine o'clock, there goes the old man."[49] His subordinates did not love him, but they respected him, and the government had every reason to feel grateful for his accomplishment. Within five years the tangled accounts of the Revolutionary period had been put in order and for the first time in years the financial records of France were up to date.[50]

Although Barbé-Marbois now served Napoleon loyally, he was privately disturbed at the severity of the censorship and the lack of free speech prevailing in the Empire. He wrote in his memoirs on July 24, 1808: "Events known throughout Europe are kept secret from all of France. It was from the English gazettes that I learned of the capture of Cadiz. It is not known even in our ports that we lost all our colonies six years ago, and if certain merchants know it they keep silent. Nevertheless, it is surmised in the interior because of the exorbitant prices to which all colonial products have risen. One does not dare to correspond, one makes no observation in public. Two friends scarcely dare to speak frankly to each other *tête-à-tête*. If a third arrives, even a friend, it is considered wise to keep silent."[51]

In February, 1812, Barbé-Marbois served again as president of the electoral college of the department of Eure. As in 1803, the business at hand was the nomination of a candidate for the Senate. It was with obvious pleasure that the president of the Cour des Comptes returned to preside at this gathering of his neighbors and fellow property owners. He had written the summer before that "evidences of the esteem of my fellow citizens will always be dear to me."[52]

Now he came out from Paris, took over the home of his friend, the prefect, who was absent, and entertained lavishly. This time the election was held in the Court of Assizes rather than the cathedral. The college comprised 294 members, but a great number of them failed to attend. The session opened on February 16 with a speech by the president assuring them of Napoleon's knowledge of the department and interest in its affairs. On the first ballot Barbé-Marbois was nominated by a vote of 159 to 1, for which he thanked the college profusely.[53]

This time Napoleon did not ignore the wishes of the department, though he waited more than a year before appointing Barbé-Marbois to a seat in the Senate. In the meantime, he had given the candidate further evidence of his favor by making him a Count of the Empire in 1813.[54] Finally, on April 5, 1813, the Emperor placed "the Count Barbé-Marbois first president of the Cour des Comptes" seventh on a list of thirteen named to the Senate. The decree described Barbé-Marbois as one "who in a few years and by assiduous labor in our Cour des Comptes has liquidated all arrears and attained the end for which we instituted it."[55]

The new senator at once won the confidence of his colleagues and soon assumed an important role in their deliberations. Napoleon's military failure in Russia in 1812 and his defeat in Germany in the autumn of 1813 forced the Emperor to consult the Senate more frequently than he had done in the years of victory. On December 20, he asked that body to nominate five men to serve with five from the Corps Législatif for the purpose of receiving communications from the throne. Barbé-Marbois was one of those named.[56] On December 28, he was one of seven chosen to act as the Grand Administrative Council for 1814.[57]

After Napoleon's defeat at Leipzig, Barbé-Marbois thought peace imperative. He was not disloyal to the Emperor yet, but he did not see how France could continue to oppose the allies. As he confided in his memoirs on December 30: "Seven great powers which march with well organized veteran armies. We will have only a few veterans and new recruits, brave but untrained, with which to oppose them."[58] The new year thus gave no prospect of being a happy one for France. Barbé-Marbois hoped for an honorable peace with the allies, but he had a foreboding that the great tragedy of the Napoleonic Empire was at hand. If so, what of the future for those who had served it?

CHAPTER IX

Minister of Louis XVIII

THE invasion of France in 1814 soon brought the end of the Empire. Despite a brilliant campaign, Napoleon lacked adequate forces to withstand the allies. His last bold stroke failed when his enemies marched straight to Paris instead of seeking a further engagement with him in the east. The Emperor's mad dash to the capital was too late, for Marshal Marmont had surrendered the city at 2:00 A. M. on March 31, just before his arrival.

The decision to ignore Napoleon's army and attack Paris was due to an overture from a party within the city led by Talleyrand. For a few days French policy was determined by this group of moderate nationalists. Some of them, like their leader, had betrayed the Emperor before his downfall. Others, like Barbé-Marbois, had remained loyal as long as a chance of victory remained. Upon the Emperor's defeat this group undertook to form a new government that would maintain the essential gains of the French Revolution and preserve the boundaries of 1789. Barbé-Marbois played an important role in these hurried deliberations. During the next two years, he served the new government in a variety of capacities, always with the hope of restoring peace and unity to the disrupted nation.

Through Czar Alexander the powers were assured that the Emperor had lost the support of France and could be deposed. A conference of Alexander and his advisers and a deputation of Frenchmen, headed by Talleyrand, resulted in the publication of a proclamation to the nation late in the evening of March 31. This document declared that the allies would not treat with Napoleon or any member of his family, offered the ancient boundaries of France, and promised to recognize a constitution drawn up by the nation. The Napoleonic Senate was convoked to name a provisional government.[1]

With the meeting of the Senate, Barbé-Marbois began to take a significant part in the organization of the new regime. That body met on April 1 under the presidency of Barbé-Marbois' old friend, the former Director Barthélemy. A provisional government of five, headed by Talleyrand, was approved at once. Barbé-Marbois was appointed on a committee with three others to consider the overthrow of Napoleon. Their report accused the Emperor of illegal and unconstitutional methods, urged his deposition, and recommended the abolition of all claims by his family to the throne of France.[2] The Senate approved on April 2, and the Corps Législatif followed suit the next day.

Barbé-Marbois became a member of a committee of five to draw up a new constitution for France. On Sunday, April 3, he and Lebrun, now the Duke of Plaisance, called on the provisional government which was meeting in Talleyrand's salon and were greeted with a request to prepare a constitution by the next morning. They naturally hesitated, complained of the lack of time, and then asked that three other senators be associated with them. The committee as thus organized met at Lebrun's the next day and began its task. They decided not to draft a complete constitution, article by article, but merely to compose a document sufficiently guaranteeing liberty, property, and an amnesty. This was read and hotly discussed on the evening of April 4 at Talleyrand's home before a group including the provisional government, Du Pont de Nemours, Fontanes, Durand, Malouet, General Du Pont, Benoît, Pasquier, Nesselrode, and Pozzo di Borgio, the last two representatives of Czar Alexander. Another project, similar to that of the committee in most respects, was also read. Quite a dispute arose over the question of heredity for the Senate. Barbé-Marbois opposed this and succeeded in defeating the proposal, but it was included the next day in the revised draft.

The constitution was read and presented to the Senate by Talleyrand on April 6. A commission was appointed to examine it and report the same day. This committee, which did not include any of those who had prepared the document in the earlier conferences, suggested certain changes, which were accepted. Barbé-Marbois opposed some of the alterations but he was not displeased with the final draft. As he wrote: "We secured the jury, liberty of the press, a firm and just government, moderate but adequate taxes, a large enough army without conscription, free commerce and navigation, retention of national domain lands by their actual possessors, a sincere and complete amnesty for everything that could awaken hatred and rekindle vengeance."[3]

France had a constitution, but who would head the new government? In the frenzied activities of late March and early April three serious contenders appeared: Napoleon's son, for whom a regency would govern until he became of age; Bernadotte, Crown Prince of Sweden but a former marshal of France; and Louis XVIII, brother of Louis XVI and the legitimate heir of the Bourbons. While the allied monarchs were deciding the fate of France, Barbé-Marbois' choice had already been made. He belonged to the moderate, liberal group of the *ancien régime*. His ideal was a monarchy surrounded by tradition, but guaranteeing the liberties of its subjects in the manner of the Constitution of 1791. In his opinion, only the Bourbons could secure these blessings for the nation. On April 5, he assembled the members of the Cour des Comptes, explained that the Senate was drafting a constitution, and declared his own adherence to the Bourbons. It was his wish rather than sober truth that led him to exclaim: "On all sides one hears the name of the Bourbons. All thoughts urge their return. They are near." It is more than distasteful to the modern ear to hear him acclaiming the foreign princes as friends and liberators: "They are today our allies, our friends, and for a long time we have not been as free as [we are] in the presence of these armed foreigners."[4] He was sailing with a full wind. The allies had decided to support the Bourbons, and the Senate voted their restoration on April 6, shortly after adopting the new constitution.

Despite his devotion to the Bourbons, Barbé-Marbois

The Chateau at Noyers

The Church and Chateau at Noyers

zealously guarded the spirit of the new constitution. It was on his advice that Talleyrand refused to verify letters patent for the Count of Artois as lieutenant general of the realm *before* Louis XVIII had accepted the senatorial constitution. "But, my Prince," he said to Taileyrand, "do not think of it. The constitution formally declares that the king, called to the throne by the Senate, will be recognized only when, on French soil, he will have sworn to and signed this constitution. It is evident that the Senate can not verify, register, or even recognize letters patent of the king anterior to the act which calls him to the throne."[5] As a compromise Artois' commission was recognized provisionally. Louis XVIII soon accepted the constitution in principle, though not in detail, and left his exile in Hartwell, England, for his new realm. Meanwhile, Napoleon had abdicated and had gone to the island of Elba, which had been given him in full sovereignty.

In May, Louis XVIII set foot in Paris for the first time since his flight on June 20, 1791. His experiences had shown him that a return to the *ancien régime* was impossible, and before entering Paris he issued the declaration of St. Ouen, promising a liberal government and the retention of the fundamental reforms of the Revolution. As soon as he was installed in the Tuileries the King appointed nine senators, nine members of the Corps Législatif, and four ministers, all moderates who had served Napoleon, to revise and redraft the constitution.[6] One of the senators was Barbé-Marbois.

The initial meeting of the commission was held on May 22. The next day the four ministers of the King brought in a proposed constitution, which was read. Barbé-Marbois opposed giving the initiative in legislation to the monarch, feeling the King would be burdened with such extensive power. He asked in vain for distribution of printed copies of the proposed constitution to the members of the commission. Sessions and further discussion of the various articles followed on May 24, 25, 26, and 28. From time to time changes were made by the King. Barbé-Marbois was perturbed by the manner in which the constitution was rushed through the committee, and his notes of the period have a tone of resignation and disappointment. "No *procès verbal* of the sessions was kept," he wrote, "and never was an act of such importance to a great nation prepared in so short a time. In the midst of the deliberation the secretary looked at the president, and on a sign passed to another article. Thus one proceeded with the constitutional act. It appears that the liberal dispositions manifested in the first days of the monarch's return are now overcome by pressure from those who surround the throne, and that already the court group is hoping to reëstablish the ancient state of things."[7]

During the eventful days of April and May, Barbé-Marbois continued undisturbed in his functions as first president of the Cour des Comptes, and this office suffered no interruption of its work in the transition from the Empire to the Restoration. On May 3, one finds the King receiving the entire Cour and listening to an address from Barbé-Marbois.[8] Several weeks later the first president protested that the recent organization of the National Guard interfered with the work of his department, and he asked that employees of the Cour des Comptes be exempted. [9]

The Charter of 1814 provided for a bicameral legislature, a Chamber of Deputies elected for a five-year term by a highly restricted franchise, and a Chamber of Peers appointed by the king. Barbé-Marbois was made a member of the upper house when the constitution was promulgated on June 4. Since the Bourbons retained the Napoleonic nobility, Barbé-Marbois entered the new house under his imperial title of count.[10] The Chamber of Peers made use of his knowledge of constitutional procedure by placing him on a committee for drafting its own rules. He acted as *rapporteur* for this committee and played a leading part in the subsequent debates.[11] He also acted as *rapporteur* for the commission on the reception and admission of new peers.[12]

In the Chamber of Peers, Barbé-Marbois upheld liberal measures and opposed the reactionary proposals of the ultra-royalist party led by the King's brother, the Count of Artois. This group desired a return to the *ancien régime* and a restoration of the property taken from the nobles and the church during the Revolution. Barbé-Marbois defended the relatively high land tax in the budget of 1814–15, which the conservatives opposed.[13] He urged against the revival of old conflicts and interference with the present ownership of property, reminding the Chamber that these matters had been settled by the Charter.[14]

At this period one finds him reporting on several projects for which his previous experience particularly qualified him. He was chairman of the commission that investigated the conditions in St. Domingue and recommended a further moratorium on debts owed by former residents of that now ruined and *de facto* independent island.[15] On November 10, he presented an extended survey of the grain trade under Napoleon, suggesting that only provisional export be permitted.[16] Barbé-Marbois successfully opposed a request of the Bank of France that it be freed from state control and on his motion a committee was appointed to examine the Bank's relation to the government.[17]

This calm parliamentary discussion of routine matters of state was but a thin façade for the growing national resentment against the Restoration. The rule of the Bourbons in 1814 was "less a government than a régime,"[18] and it seemed that the ultras would succeed in reversing the work of the Revolution. The former officers of Napoleon were furious over their retirement from the army on half pay. From his island exile the Emperor shrewdly judged the situation and planned his return. Exactly eleven months after his marshals had surrendered Paris he again set foot on French soil. Three weeks later Louis XVIII fled to Belgium and Napoleon entered the capital.

Like all other prominent Frenchmen, the first president of the Cour des Comptes was sorely puzzled as to his course in this crisis. His son-in-law rallied to the Emperor and his daughter was an outspoken Bonapartist even after the Hundred Days. Barbé-Marbois' conduct is not clear. Napoleon is said to have referred to him as one who had revealed "an ingratitude that not even necessity could justify."[19] The Emperor is reputed to have refused his former minister an interview,[20] and there is no evidence that they saw each other during the Hundred Days. Barbé-Marbois was relieved of his office at the Cour des Comptes, and Collin de Sussy replaced him.

Whatever his innermost thoughts may have been, Barbé-Marbois' outer conduct was so prudent that he retained the fullest confidence of the Bourbons. He retired to Noyers and gave his time to agriculture and letters. Years before as a young secretary in Philadelphia he had spoken of writing an account of the treason of Benedict Arnold. What better and safer flight from reality could he find in the summer of 1815? The volume was soon finished and was published the following year.[21] Jefferson, to whom the author sent a copy, said it threw "light on that incident of history which we did not possess before."[22]

The book is most significant today for its reflection of Barbé-Marbois' knowledge and interest in American affairs. After thirty years' absence from the United States he felt her revolution to be "the most remarkable" in history and thought the peculiar conditions of this country would guarantee its good effects forever. His tribute to the American Constitution deserves a place with the later comments of de Tocqueville and Bryce. The fathers of that document, he wrote, "had attempted what the greatest philosophers, both ancient and modern, had proposed only as theories easier to imagine than to realize. They passed the boundaries that Aristotle, Bodin, More, and Harrington had feared to cross. Before quitting this life they were themselves the witnesses of the perfect success of this great enterprise."

Tucked away in the preface of this book is Barbé-Marbois' theory of social change. Here he states succinctly the principles that guided his entire political life. Reformers, he said, should not try to "go ahead of their day. They should cast a favorable eye on only those changes which time and increased knowledge bring inevitably, and despite all opposition. This way is slow but sure. It is dangerous to hasten it but equally perilous to attempt to arrest its progress."[23]

After the defeat of Napoleon at Waterloo on June 18, Barbé-Marbois took a renewed interest in French politics. His notes give a brief glimpse of the national perplexity about the choice of a future sovereign. Napoleon abdicated in favor of his son on June 22, and a provisional government was set up under Fouché, former priest, former Jacobin, and former Imperial minister of police. The generals were uncertain about their future course. The chambers at first accepted Napoleon II and a regency, but by June 27 the allies' opposition had rendered this impossible. There was then talk of a desperate rally to Napoleon, a republic, the Duke of Orleans, Louis XVIII on condition that the others abdicate, and finally Eugène de Beauharnais.[24]

Louis XVIII turned the scales in his favor by returning on the heels of the conquering armies. Paris capitulated on July 3 and the King was in the Tuileries on July 8. He proceeded upon the theory that he was the rightful king of France and that his rule had never been interrupted. Former officials who had been loyal to him resumed their places in the administration. It was thus that Barbé-Marbois returned from Noyers to his position at the Cour des Comptes.

In August, the King asked Barbé-Marbois to preside at

the electoral college of the department of Bas-Rhin meeting in Strasbourg. His Lorraine origin and his knowledge of German were probably the reasons for the appointment. The mission was an important one and presented unusual difficulties. The East was occupied by Russian, Prussian, and Bavarian troops, and the city itself was surrounded by Austrians. There was some talk to the effect that France would be forced to cede Alsace and Lorraine as the price of supporting Napoleon a second time. It was being suggested that the Meuse, the Vosges, the Saône, and the Rhone, rather than the Rhine, were the natural frontiers of the country. Barbé-Marbois thought Austria would have seized Alsace if the restoration of Louis XVIII had been followed by an insurrection in the province. Prussia actually desired a partition of France but the British and Russians vigorously opposed it. In the end the actual territorial loss in the treaty of 1815 was slight.

Barbé-Marbois informed Talleyrand from Strasbourg of the measures he had taken in the department. He had discouraged all ideas of dismemberment, reassured those fearful of the consequences of the Restoration, and placated the Protestants, who were especially attached to Napoleon and uneasy over the religious consequences of the return of the Bourbons. The good will of the Protestants was important, as they controlled the banking interests of Alsace. The election was held without disorder and three Protestants and four Catholics were nominated, two of them being members of the recent Napoleonic chamber.[25]

The elections of 1815 resulted in an *ultra* victory in the country as a whole, and the new chamber, christened the *introuvable,* was more royalist than the King himself. The Talleyrand-Fouché ministry, which had negotiated the second Restoration, was succeeded by a moderate, but more royalist, government led by the Duc de Richelieu, a wise aristocrat who had spent his exile as governor of the Crimea for Alexander I. Barbé-Marbois was offered the ministry of justice and, after some hesitancy due to his advanced age, he accepted the post. "M. de Richelieu, who attached great importance to having him for a colleague, on account of his reputation for strict integrity, pressed him to accept office so much, that he complied saying that the insistence of the Duc de Richelieu did him such honour that he would gladly agree."[26]

The new minister retained François Guizot, later one of the most distinguished Frenchmen of the century, as his chief subordinate.[27] Their collaboration was a happy one and Guizot characterized Barbé-Marbois at this time as one who "belonged to that old France which, in a spirit of generous liberality, had adopted and upheld, with enlightened moderation, the principles most cherished by the France of the day."[28]

Rarely, even in France, has a minister of justice faced so trying a situation as that which greeted Barbé-Marbois in the autumn of 1815. The Hundred Days had added heat to passions already at the boiling point. The *ultras,* supported by allied bayonets, were livid with rage at the Bonapartists and inhuman in their demands for vengeance. The King and the ministry favored a moderate course, but they could not refuse some concessions to the majority in the Chamber of Deputies. Four laws were speedily adopted in an attempt to punish the rebels and guard the new government from its Revolutionary and Bonapartist enemies.[29] All these measures pertained to the work of the minister of justice but those concerning "seditious cries" and the *cours prévôtales* were considered sufficiently important to be introduced by Barbé-Marbois himself.

The law on "seditious cries," primarily the work of Guizot,[30] proposed imprisonment from three months to five years, with subsequent loss of civic rights from five to ten years, for those who attacked the government by cries, speeches, or seditious writing. Deportation was provided for a few offenses. The bill, as introduced by Barbé-Marbois, on October 16,[31] was entirely too moderate for the *ultras,* who proceeded to alter it drastically. The Chamber of Deputies substituted the death penalty for deportation in major offenses and made punishable by deportation all threats against the royal family. A motion to apply the death penalty for carrying the tricolor, now outlawed in favor of the ancient *fleur de lis,* failed by a narrow margin to pass the Chamber. Barbé-Marbois pictured the horrors of his own exile in Guiana so vividly that the Chamber was induced to permit deportation, rather than the death penalty, for more offenses than it had intended originally.[32] Otherwise the minister accepted the amendments to the law. A contemporary historian described Barbé-Marbois' speech in defense of the revised bill before the Chamber of Peers in biting terms: "Never has one accumulated more lies to make the condition of our country look black."[33]

During the debates on "seditious cries" the Chamber of Deputies demanded the reëstablishment of the *cours prévô-*

tales, for which authority could be found under Article 63 of the constitution. These special courts were heirs to those organized under the criminal code of 1808, which had jurisdiction over vagabondage, rebellion by armed force, armed smuggling, counterfeiting, assassinations by armed bands, and thefts or acts of violence by soldiers. Very reluctantly Barbé-Marbois agreed to present a law for their renewal. This measure, too, was once thought to have been the work of Guizot, but recent research shows that it was prepared entirely by Barbé-Marbois and the director of criminal affairs.[34] When asked by Louis XVIII when the bill would be ready for introduction, the minister is said to have replied: "Sire, I am ashamed to tell Your Majesty that it is already prepared."[35] To the offenses envisaged by the Code of 1808, the new law added seditious meetings, assumption of command of a force or garrison without authority, and all crimes under the recently enacted law on seditious cries. The courts were composed of a president, four judges chosen from the ordinary magistrates, and a *prévôt* (hence the name of the courts), who would be at least a colonel in rank. A court was set up in each department. Barbé-Marbois attempted to moderate the administration of this law which he secretly opposed, and his first instructions to the new courts were couched in a very tolerant spirit.[36]

While minister of justice, Barbé-Marbois also retained his position as first president of the Cour des Comptes. On October 16 he introduced a bill in the Chamber of Peers proposing the reduction of this court from three chambers to two. Since the nation had suffered great loss of territory with the fall of the Empire, this was a commendable measure dictated by economy and common sense. The Peers accepted it without difficulty and all the provisions were approved individually as they were considered in the Chamber of Deputies, but the entire measure was rejected on the final vote in the lower house.[37] The opposition was primarily personal, for the *ultras* were already displeased with Barbé-Marbois' moderate policies. They had acquiesced in his appointment because of his reputation for royalism,[38] but they soon found his views quite out of keeping with their own. The rejection of this measure reorganizing the Cour des Comptes was the first move in their campaign to secure his dismissal from the ministry.

The escape of Count Lavalette from the Conciergie on December 21, 1815, led to an onslaught by the *ultras* against Barbé-Marbois and Decazes, the minister of police.[39] Lavalette had been postmaster under the Empire, and on March 20, 1814, he had taken possession of the general post office, in the name of Napoleon, a few hours before the arrival of the Emperor in Paris. For this he had been tried and condemned to death. Repeated pleas for his pardon were refused, even though Richelieu himself desired to save him. The Countess therefore prepared a daring escape for her husband. When she and her daughter called on him the evening prior to the date set for his execution she changed clothes with the Count, who then took the hand of their daughter and walked out unmolested. On January 9, 1816, he crossed the Belgian frontier in the guise of an English officer.[40] The day following the escape a motion was introduced in the Chamber of Deputies calling on Decazes and Barbé-Marbois for an explanation of the affair.

A committee, appointed to investigate, proposed an address to the King requesting the removal of the two ministers. The King's sympathies lay with the ministry rather than the *ultras* and he refused the petition. A dismissal would have been an acknowledgment of ministerial responsibility to the Chamber of Deputies, and thus a victory for the latter in one of the chief constitutional conflicts of the Restoration. The monarch deftly replied that the only way to test the nation's confidence in the ministers would be through a national election.[41] As the chamber did not care to appeal to the electorate, Barbé-Marbois was saved from the vengeance of his enemies for a few months more.

Among the minister's manifold duties were some interesting affairs concerning the executed Bourbons. He corresponded with the prefect of the Seine and the Chamber of Deputies regarding the mourning to be worn on January 21, the anniversary of the death of Louis XVI.[42] In April, copies of a letter of Marie Antoinette's and of the will of Louis XVI were sent to the *Procureurs Généraux*.[43] Much more spectacular was the exhumation of the remains of the Duc d'Enghien. On the evening of his execution, March 21, 1804, the body of that unfortunate prince had been thrown into a hastily made grave by the wall of the fortress at Vincennes. Louis XVIII asked Barbé-Marbois to appoint a commission for exhumation and this was accomplished on March 21, 1816, the twelfth anniversary of the tragic deed.[44] The body was reinterred in the church in the chateau and a suitable monument raised in d'Enghien's honor.[45]

Devotion to the Bourbons, however, was not allowed to interfere with the routine of judicial business. The Duchess of Berry, wife of the King's nephew, took an extended tour in the south and center of the country and certain of the courts planned to greet her in the larger cities through which she passed. Barbé-Marbois wrote to the presidents of the royal courts at Nimes and Bourges: "I can only applaud the sentiments manifested by the court on this occasion, but I recommend to you however to take the necessary precautions, in conjunction with the *Procureur Général* in order that this expedition may not interfere with the completion of trials. It is by rendering justice zealously and speedily that magistrates can best prove their devotion to the king."[46] Good words, even if the author did expect the monarch to see them!

In the spring of 1816 the *ultras* turned the full force of their attack on Barbé-Marbois. His opposition to a return to the *ancien régime* and his moderate administration of their reactionary legislation made him particularly odious to them. Richelieu was anxious to rid himself of Vaublanc, minister of the interior, who had become a supporter of the Artois faction. In order to quiet the anticipated opposition to Vaublanc's removal, he decided to part with Barbé-Marbois at the same time.[47] On May 8, both men were relieved of their ministries. Guizot, as Marbois' secretary general, was also dismissed. Poor health was the public reason given for Marbois' removal. He had been ill, but at this particular time he was better than he had been for months. As he said, his physician told him he was well, but the decree of the King stated he was worse.

Guizot thought Marbois was "upright and well-informed . . . but neither quick sighted nor commanding. . . .

He had opposed the reaction with more integrity than energy and served the king with dignity without acquiring personal influence."[48] In other words, he was a moderate in an era of unusual bitterness. For the moment there was no place in the ministry for a great compromiser.

CHAPTER X

The Marquis de Marbois

ALTHOUGH Barbé-Marbois was seventy-one on his dismissal from the ministry, more than a score of useful years remained for him. Nature had endowed him with a strong body and he had conserved his health by temperate living, regular exercise, and steady work.[1] To this physical virility he joined a mental energy that defied senility. In the leisure of these later years he continued his old interests and developed new ones, participating in humanitarian enterprises, writing several books, and superintending his estates. He was, in truth, a cultivated gentleman of the Restoration.

Yet these wide interests did not interfere with his public duties. At an age when most men have retired, he resumed the active direction of the Cour des Comptes, from which he had never resigned as first president. This institution is Marbois' monument, his claim to a permanent place in the administrative history of modern France. He organized the Cour in 1807 and, except for the Hundred Days, continued as its head for twenty-seven years. Until the reforms of Leon Blum's first ministry, 1936–37, the Cour des Comptes remained almost exactly as Marbois conceived it. Perhaps no institution in contemporary France has changed so little since the days of Napoleon.

Marbois insisted upon the strictest devotion to duty by all his subordinates and set them a high example. He arrived punctually at his office in the morning and never permitted anything to interfere with the daily routine. The Cour was open for business as usual during every day of the July Revolution. Despite the changes of government from 1807 to 1834 the accounts of the state were always kept up to date. There was never any reason to complain of the work of the Cour des Comptes. The first president used all his influence to secure economy in expenditures and to oppose borrowing. His contemporaries "listened to him with the respect that Greece gave to old Nestor."[2]

A stern disciplinarian is never loved by those under him, and such was the case with Marbois. His associates at the Cour respected his integrity and his ability but resented his manner. This was particularly true in Marbois' later years when he seemed more dictatorial than patriarchal. It is interesting to quote one of his critics: "In the eyes of the Cour, Monsieur the Marquis de Marbois sat less as president than absolute master. ... M. de Marbois had organized the Cour des Comptes; he understood its great importance, but he feared the influence of the able and hard-working magistrates who composed it, since the regulation issued by the first president on December 1, 1807, decreed that the general assemblies [of the Court] should not have any deliberative power."[3]

New honors soon came to the former minister. Louis

XVIII dismissed the Chamber of Deputies on September 5, 1816, and in the new election secured a majority of constitutional royalists and moderates. Thus freed from the domination of the *ultras,* the monarch found it possible to reward some of their enemies, even so prominent a one as Barbé-Marbois. The monarch accorded him an annual pension of twenty thousand francs to be paid from the funds of the ministry of justice. To the surprise of his enemies, no doubt, the recipient declined the gift. "I have much desired," he wrote the minister of justice, "a testimonial of the satisfaction of the king for my public services during more than fifty years. The ordinance of His Majesty contains this recognition. I am deeply grateful for it. But happy with the honor contained in this act of the king's generosity I propose not to accept its other dispositions until my advanced age will no longer permit me to fulfil the functions of First President of the Cour des Comptes." Louis XVIII conveyed his personal appreciation of Barbé-Marbois' attitude[4] and soon gave further evidence of his favor. He was raised in the peerage from the title of "Count" to that of "Marquis," his letters patent being registered in Paris on May 2, 1818.[5] He was known henceforth as the Marquis de Marbois. In 1816, he had been elected to the Institute, division of inscriptions and belles-lettres. He became a member of the councils of public education, hospitals, and prisons, interesting himself actively in all these branches of the government service.

Despite his work at the Cour des Comptes, Marbois took an active part in the deliberations of the Chamber of Peers, particularly in the years 1819–28. His greatest interest was finance, and he seems to have served constantly on the committee for consideration of the budget. Members of the chamber were given leave to print their speeches and reports, as is the custom today in the American Congress, and more than sixty such pamphlets were published for Marbois between 1814 and 1830.[6] A friend described his addresses in the chamber as "liberal and moderate, his words grave and austere, but appreciative of circumstances [and] respectful of the conscience of his political opponents."[7]

On August 25, 1818, the Marquis happily completed a project he had sponsored since the early days of the Restoration. During the Revolution the famous statue of Henry IV on the Pont Neuf had been overturned and broken. In 1814, Marbois assembled ten notables who made him their president in a campaign to restore this statue of the first Bourbon. The necessary sum was raised by private subscription,[8] and the day of the unveiling was a great occasion for Marbois, who made the chief address. He recounted the services of Henry IV, who died before he could complete his work. Then turning to Louis XVIII he delivered a charge full of flattery, but with a warning for the future. "More fortunate, Sire," he exclaimed, "you have given your people a favorable Charter. It is establishing itself under your eyes, already its advantages are apparent. A public spirit is forming, opinions are being clarified, laws are obeyed better, and from one end of the kingdom to the other this Charter, received with joy, operates without opposition. Sustain, Sire, sustain this fruit of your wisdom in order that a grateful France may enjoy stable government and prosperity during

Your Majesty's reign."[9] Had the successor of Louis XVIII heeded this counsel the Bourbons might be ruling in France today.

Marbois was one of the most active members of the Royal Society for Prison Reform founded by Louis XVIII. In 1819 and 1823, he visited certain departments in Normandy and published reports which threw valuable light upon prison conditions in that area.[10] In the earlier visit he found the food poor; although the law prescribed bread and soup, the latter was served in only a few places. The term "bread and water" had only too real a meaning for the unfortunates he met within the prison walls. The bread was distributed every other day in some places and the famished inmates often ate two days' supply at once. Marbois tasted the bread in all the prisons he visited; it was universally soggy and sometimes only partially cooked. Despite the terrible food, Marbois admitted that a vast improvement in prison conditions had occurred in the preceding half century. Better housing was provided in the former monasteries and convents, some of which had been converted into prisons following the suppression of monasticism in 1790. Only a few dungeons with wet floors and men chained to the walls remained, and Marbois urged their immediate abolition. He found all the prisoners, however, suffering from lack of exercise, and he recommended employment for them. Bedding was deplorable, generally straw on the floor, and beds and linen were needed nearly everywhere. A large, centralized prison had been constructed at Gaillon, and this was well run. The prisoners were employed and given some pay for their work. The investigator reserved his highest praise for the prisons of Rouen, which were humanely administered and had begun reforms even before the organization of the Royal Society.

On his return visit four years later Marbois found a number of improvements in these prisons. Criminals were treated according to law and not after the personal, and often vindictive, whims of their jailers. Prisoners had better beds, soup every day, and meat twice a week. At Gaillon he talked with all the inmates who desired to see him. None of them claimed to be there contrary to law or from the vengeance of an enemy. Punishments for minor offenses, however, were absurd. At Gaillon he found a lad of fourteen condemned to thirteen months' imprisonment for stealing nuts. Others had stolen only a few potatoes, and most of the 469 young people, between sixteen and twenty-five, in this prison were guilty of small thefts. He urged that minor offenders and young people, especially, be separated from hardened criminals. The law should be revised, too, but the judges could be more lenient with youth. He vigorously opposed the suggested introduction of the treadmill, recently invented in England and so widely used there for mutinous prisoners. He felt France should discontinue rather than augment her machines of torture.

Marbois' deep interest in prison reform was due partly, no doubt, to his own experiences in Guiana. Certainly this explains his public opposition to that country as a colony for Europeans, which drew a sarcastic book in reply,[11] and his campaign to abolish deportation as a legal punishment. In 1826–27 there was some trouble in the country with liberated criminals who had served sentences at hard labor, and the councils of forty-one departments petitioned the government for the effective application of the law permitting deportation, which had presently fallen into desuetude.[12] Marbois was asked to respond to this by publishing the journal of his own deportation. But he thought this would confuse the immediate issue, and he wrote a pamphlet[13] omitting all reference to 18 Fructidor. He cited the case of the British penal colony at Botany Bay, Australia, as an example of the problems convicts caused. His pamphlet was distributed in the departments and aided materially in silencing the demand for the effective application of deportation, though Marbois failed in his campaign to remove the law from the code.

Despite his feud with the *ultras* in 1815–16, Marbois experienced no embarrassment when their royal leader, Artois, succeeded Louis XVIII in 1824 under the title of Charles X. He continued in his office at the Cour des Comptes and enjoyed the best of relations with the new monarch. For his part Marbois gave the King no reason to complain. His loyalty was almost excessive. On the two occasions annually when the Cour des Comptes was received at court as a body the first president passed all limits in his flattery of Charles X. His address at the New Year's reception in 1825 exceeded the bounds of good taste: "A thousand times happy is this day when, received in the royal palace, we find wisdom seated on the throne and the sceptre in the hands of justice."[14]

Marbois' interest and sympathy for the United States deepened as the young republic prospered and expanded. He welcomed the purchase of Florida in 1819 and wrote

President Monroe that no American had received the acquisition with more enthusiasm than he.[15] His home was a meeting place for Americans in Paris, and he often rendered them special courtesies, particularly when they came recommended by his old friends of American revolutionary days.[16]

In 1822, Marbois conceived the idea of writing a history of the Louisiana cession, including an introductory essay on the contemporary government of the United States. He informed Monroe of his plan and requested any available papers and books that might assist his research.[17] The American president did not reply until February 10, 1824.[18] He seemed chiefly concerned to establish his old contention that Napoleon's decision to sell Louisiana had been greatly influenced by his own arrival in France, thus according little credit to Livingston for the successful conclusion of the negotiations. Monroe did forward two published volumes of *State Papers* through the new American minister to France, James Brown, who was leaving for his post. Brown, who had met Marbois in 1818, found the Marquis extremely well disposed toward the United States. He characterized the recent presidential address stating the Monroe Doctrine as "not only the *best* but the *best timed* state paper he had ever read and he hoped Europe would be benefited by the check it might give to a career contrary to her own true policy and best interests." Marbois regretted the current coolness in America toward France and the leaning toward Great Britain.[19] In acknowledging the *State Papers,* Marbois observed that the more he continued with the research for his book the more he was convinced that good relations between France and the United States were essential for the progress of civilization and the prosperity of the world. He realized that an alliance was both impossible and undesirable, but he thought the two nations could cooperate as friends.[20]

The Marbois-Monroe correspondence about Louisiana brought Brown into contact with Marbois on a number of occasions. The American minister was amazed at the role of such an old man. "The vigor of intellect, and fine flow of spirits which Mr. Marbois possesses at his advanced age," he wrote, "are really extraordinary. He continues to take a very active part in public affairs and is highly respected for the probity of his character and the soundness of his judgment."[21] Two years later Monroe, then in retirement on his estate in Virginia, sent Marbois a memoir and some documents concerning his own public career, including his two missions to France.[22] On presenting these papers the American minister was more impressed than ever by the elder stateman's good health and quick intellect. "It gives me great pleasure to inform you," he reported, "that this extraordinary man still preserves his intellects in their full vigor at eighty-two years and is unquestionably the most active intelligent and useful statesman in France. How strange it is, that amidst all the revolutions which have taken place within the last thirty-seven years, he has preserved his life, his intellects, his fortune, and his reputation."[23]

The exchange of letters with Monroe afforded Marbois an opportunity to express frankly his opinion of their era. "We became acquainted in difficult times," he mused.

"They have ceased for your country but I cannot say as much for Europe. She has grown older, and it was possible to hope for a while that she would be rejuvenated. Bonaparte could have given his name to our century if he had been capable of loving liberty under wise laws. But he insanely thought himself wiser than others and loved liberty only for himself. He has left imitators. Your country is the despair of despots. I will not live to see them profit from the lesson [of America], but sooner or later the world will do it."[24]Marbois had just finished the history of the Louisiana cession, but he stated that he was uncertain whether he would publish it during his lifetime or leave it to his executors. The doubt arose from the generous way in which he had spoken of the liberal institutions of America. The unfavorable comparison with France which readers would inevitably make might prove embarrassing for a servant of Charles X.

The volume had been in manuscript over a year when the American historian, Jared Sparks, arrived in Paris for the purpose of consulting historical documents relative to the life of Washington and the history of the American Revolution. Sparks was probably the first historical scholar from the United States ever to work in the Paris archives, and it was only by the intervention of influential Frenchmen that he could secure the privileges he desired. Quite naturally he appealed to Marbois, well known for his friendship to Sparks' compatriots. Marbois wrote the minister of foreign affairs on July 12, 1828, and was told that Sparks should indicate the documents he required, which, in fact, the historian had already done.[25] Marbois also requested

M. LE M.⁹ BARBÉ DE MARBOIS,

Pair de France.

The Marquis in his Later Years

Engraving by Ambroise Tardieu

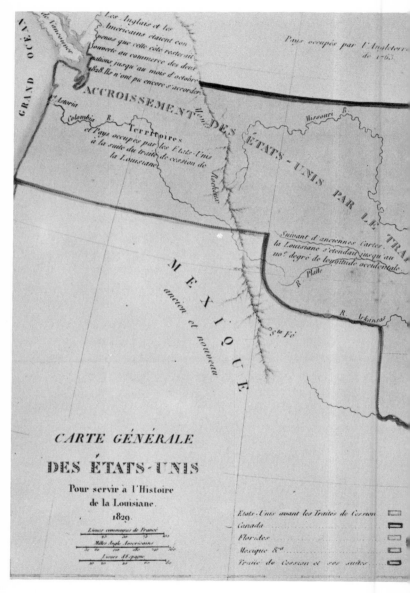

The United States in 1829, showing the territory acquired by the Louisiana Treaty of 1803, the Rush-Bagot Agreement with Great Britain in 1818, and the Transcontinental Treaty with Spain in 1819.

From François Barbé-Marbois, *Histoire de La Louisiane et de La Cession de Cette Colonie par La France aux États-Unis de L'Amérique Septentrionale* (Paris, 1829).

Caricature of Barbé-Marbois

by Daumier, May 28, 1835

permission for Sparks to work in the archives of the war and navy departments, which was granted.[26]

While Sparks was waiting for the necessary ministerial authorizations to pursue his research, Marbois asked him to read and criticize his manuscript history of Louisiana.[27] Undoubtedly Sparks' enthusiastic reaction was an important factor in Marbois' decision to publish the book immediately. When the American presented his written critique on August 27, he urged the author to place his work before the public and offered his services for its distribution in the United States. Sparks was then editor of *The North American Review* and he generously proposed to use its columns for advertising the book to his fellow citizens. He also offered to superintend the translation and publication of the volume in America, and Marbois accepted his services.[28] The book was published in Paris in 1829 and an American edition appeared the following year.[29]

The *Histoire de la Louisiane* was a remarkable achievement for a man of eighty-four still busily engaged in public life. The book had four parts: a hundred-page description of the Constitution and government of the United States, a history of the French and Spanish regimes in Louisiana, an account of the cession to the United States, and the story of the transfer of the colony. The argument was supported by forty-seven pages of pertinent documents. The text was well organized, the style lucid and virile.[30]

The author accurately sketched the main events in the history of Louisiana from its foundation to its successful defense against the British by Andrew Jackson in 1815. The account of the Spanish period derived special value from Marbois' residence in the United States and St. Domingue from 1779 to 1790. Brief discussions of Franco-American relations were inserted in proper chronological order. The governments of the French Revolution, especially the Directory, were criticized for their lack of tact and understanding in dealing with the United States. Marbois' version of the negotiations with Livingston and Monroe was thoroughly accurate, but one may question his statement that Napoleon sold Louisiana to keep it from falling into the hands of Great Britain.[31]

Posterity's interest in the events of 1803 has obscured the significance of the volume as a description of the United States in the 1820's. Marbois' picture of American institutions was very flattering; the only adverse criticism concerned slavery, which he feared would eventually destroy the Union. The sectional issue had been well dramatized by the Missouri Compromise, which he recounted. As noted before, he prophesied a population of one hundred million whites for the nation by 1900. He commended the moderate government expenses and said public finances were much better handled than in Europe. In the lengthy review which Sparks accorded the French edition in the *North American Review*,[32] he spoke enthusiastically of the author's acute appreciation of this country, crediting the book with "a wider knowledge and more accurate views of the government, institutions, progress, and political wisdom of the United States, than any other which has appeared from a European hand. . . . Although the author touches upon a great number and variety of subjects, relating to our civil and political condition, we know not how he could have been more accurate in his facts or just in his reflections, or enlightened in his opinions, even if he had lived among us; and the citizen of the United States must be a fastidious patriot indeed, who is not charmed with the tone of candor and spirit of liberality which everywhere pervades his remarks."

Monroe was so slow in acknowledging his copy of the *Histoire de la Louisiane* that Marbois wrote asking whether it had arrived.[33] Several months later he received a brief, and cool, reply. "I consider it an able work," Monroe wrote, "written in a spirit of candour, and justice to all the parties, and of kind feelings to me, yet there were some points in the negotiation which have escaped your attention, respecting which I will write you hereafter. I have lately been much indisposed, and although now relieved from fever yet am too weak to enter into the subject. Too much time has since elapsed for you to recollect every incident and detail."[34] The difficulty was that Monroe felt he should have been given more credit for the successful conclusion of the negotiations.[35] There is no evidence that he ever corresponded further with Marbois.

Sparks had found the Marquis hale and active during his visits to France. The two men dined together on occasion, and Marbois rendered his American friend a number of special courtesies such as an invitation to a session of the Royal Academy of Inscriptions and Belles Lettres at the Institute.[36] Not only did Marbois attend to his duties at the Cour des Comptes, but he was "one of the most active members of the House of Peers, constant in his attendance, and taking a lively interest in all the political movements of the day."[37] However, the records of the chamber do not mention him in 1829. He was stricken by a serious illness during that winter and it was felt he could not survive.[38] But his strong constitution withstood the attack and in the spring of 1830 he was himself again. Hardly had he resumed his duties when France experienced another revolution, this time the last one in Marbois' long career.

On July 26, Charles X issued four ordinances dissolving a recently elected Chamber of Deputies before it could meet, ordering new elections, modifying the electoral system, and establishing a censorship of the press. All were contrary to the spirit of the constitution, and the last two were clear violations of the very letter of that document. The King and his ministers were totally unprepared for the joint insurrection of the *bourgeoisie* and working classes which soon passed into a revolution. The middle class was itself startled by the demand for a republic that arose from the boulevards. In the crisis of the revolution, Thiers skillfully directed the selection of the Duc d'Orleans as successor to Charles X. Orleans was chosen lieutenant general of the realm on July 30 and popularly recognized the following day in a dramatic appearance at the Hotel de Ville, when he displayed the tricolor and received the kiss of Lafayette, whom the republicans had hoped to make president. The charter was revised to suit the middle class and on August 9 Orleans mounted the throne as Louis Philippe, King of the French.

Like nearly everyone else, Marbois was completely unprepared for the sudden deposition of the elder branch of the Bourbons. As late as July 18, he had presented an ad-

dress on behalf of the Cour des Comptes congratulating
Charles X on the victories of his armies in Algeria, just
being acquired by France. Once again he demonstrated his
ability to adapt himself advantageously to a new situation.
He and his colleagues acquiesced to the change of dynasty
with good grace and on August 5 Marbois presented a flattering address to the Lieutenant General from the Cour.
The first president rejoiced in the good fortune that had
called to the throne one surrounded with such a large
family, the "promise of a happy future." Louis Philippe
received the Cour for the first time as a reigning monarch
on August 20, Marbois again presenting the tribute of his
colleagues. By the New Year's reception the Marquis had
found again the flowing words with which he formerly
addressed the elder Bourbons.[39] "What can we add to the
acclamations of gratitude and joy of all France," he said
to the King. "Father of the country! This is the splendid
title which the love of Frenchmen has just chosen for you."
Louis Philippe confirmed Marbois' positions at the Cour
des Comptes and in the Chamber of Peers, and the Marquis' relations with the new dynasty were as amicable as
they had been with the old one. In 1832 he was invited to
serve as a witness to the marriage of Princess Louise to
Leopold I, King of the Belgians.[40]

Two years later Marbois retired from the Cour des
Comptes. Evidence is somewhat contradictory regarding
the circumstances. He was ill in 1833 and submitted his
resignation, which was not accepted by the King, though
it remained in his hands.[41] According to one story, Marbois
learned on April 4, 1834, that Louis Philippe planned to use

the resignation, whereupon the Marquis stated that he could be removed only through a new one, which he then presented.[42] Marbois himself makes no reference to such negotiations, attributing his retirement to failing eyesight.[43] The monarch was very gracious in the letter he wrote on April 4 accepting the resignation. He referred to his own exile in the United States at the time when Marbois had been in Guiana and stated that his regard for the Marquis had increased during the brief time they had served together in the Chamber of Peers. Finally, Louis Philippe sent Marbois his portrait as a mark of his gratitude and respect.[44] The first president assembled the Cour on April 5 and read the exchange of letters the previous day with the monarch. In a moving scene Marbois then took leave of his colleagues, most of them associates for more than twenty years.

After his retirement from the Cour des Comptes, the Marquis made but one further appearance in public life. In April, 1834, serious insurrections broke out against Louis Philippe in Lyons and Paris and were put down with difficulty. The following May, 121 prisoners captured in these two cities were arraigned in a trial before the Chamber of Peers. Outside the Luxembourg Palace, where the trial was held, a hostile mob heckled the Peers, tried to bar entrance to the building, and almost precipitated an open attack on the chamber.[45] Marbois, now ninety, achieved notoriety by having himself carried through the hostile crowd by his servants.[46] His harsh attitude toward the prisoners and his staunch support of the repressive measures which were enacted into law in September earned him the animosity of the liberals. Daumier drew a bitter caricature of him.

Freed from the cares of office Marbois yielded to the oft-expressed wishes of his friends and published the journal of his deportation to Guiana. This work, already cited, included an account of 18 Fructidor, Marbois' exile, and long sections on the climate, vegetation, history, and peoples of Guiana, especially the Indians. The author stated that the journal was published just as written in 1797–99. About this same time Marbois also compiled a list of the offices he had filled during his life, giving a few brief comments on his public career.

During his later years Marbois made generous donations to the commune of Noyers and the adjacent Norman territory in which his property lay. Most of the gifts remained anonymous until after his death. Because of his service on the council of public education he was especially interested in the local schools. In 1825, he rebuilt the schoolhouse at Noyers and gave two acres of land as an endowment for it. Each September the schoolmaster was to bring a handful of stalks of wheat and specimens of the handwriting of the three best penmen in the school and present them to Madame Lebrun at the chateau.[47] The Commune received other grants for the repair of roads, the maintenance of fountains and public washplaces, and the repair of roofs.

Outside of Noyers, Marbois contributed seventy-seven thousand francs to the *arrondissement,* between 1832 and 1835, for education and the installation of non-inflammable roofs.[48] The latter was one of his chief rural interests.

The thatched roofs, however picturesque they may seem to a modern tourist, were a constant fire hazard, and Marbois delighted in seeing the peasants cover their houses with tile. In 1836 Marbois made an anonymous gift of sixteen thousand francs to the flood victims of the area.

Although with advancing age he came less frequently to Noyers, the proprietor kept vigorous watch over the care of his estate. His interest in agriculture continued to the end. He was the first person in the region to have a threshing machine. An apple, *la Marboise,* was named for him. His farm was a model, his fields the best cultivated in the neighborhood, and the unused acres were all forested.[49] No lover of the soil could ask more than this.

Despite his prosperity and success in public affairs, Marbois' private life was not happy. Noyers, though a beautiful rural retreat, also sheltered the great tragedy of his career. Sometime after her husband's deportation to Guiana, Madame Marbois lost her mind. The popular story is that she went mad with worry over his exile, but it is impossible today to discover the details of the case or to determine just when she became insane. She was placed in a house adjacent to the chateau and there she lingered a pathetic figure until January 28, 1834. Marbois described his wife's condition on April 20, 1829, in a letter to Richard Willing, the husband of her niece: "The illness of Madame de Marbois has not ceased; however, she is calm. She lives in the country in a spot that I have made as agreeable as I could. All her desires are granted immediately."[50] Little but tragedy had dogged her footsteps since the night she and her husband precipitously fled from St. Domingue. Not once after that did she see her native Philadelphia or the members of her immediate family.

Before Marbois' death there were already evidences of the subsequent flighty and tragic conduct of his daughter. As a young woman she had been a noted beauty and a universal favorite. Her high spirit and quick intelligence made her the best of company. American visitors to the Marbois home almost invariably spoke of her in the most enthusiastic terms. At first her marriage to Charles-François-Paul Lebrun seemed ideal. Both young people were attractive and the match united two families of similar interests and long association. A daughter, named Elisa for her grandmother, was born of this union. Sometime during the Restoration, Madame Lebrun became restless. She championed the Greeks in their war of independence and traveled extensively in Italy, Greece, and the Near East. In 1831, she was granted a legal separation from her husband.[51] Her father was fortunately saved the embarrassment occasioned by her later conduct.[52] Lebrun remained a fast and loyal friend of his father-in-law, both men apparently agreeing that Sophie was mentally unbalanced. While Madame Lebrun was traveling in Syria in 1837 her daughter became ill and died at Beirut.

Marbois was spared this last shock, for a few weeks before, he, too, had ended his long life. On January 12, 1837, he died in Paris at 1 Place de la Madeleine, where he had lived since his resignation from the Cour des Comptes. It was fitting that his funeral should be held in the Madeleine Church, which as minister of the treasury he had helped to finish. Though Lebrun was the only member of his family present, official France paid great honor to its departed colleague. A deputation from the Chamber of Peers, all the members of the Cour des Comptes, and a delegation from the Institute rendered homage to the deceased. Active pall bearers were the Duc de Broglie, formerly prime minister; Count Portalis, the famous jurist; Baron Silvestre de Sacy, and Viscount d'Aboncourt, who replaced M. Barthe, the ailing first president of the Cour des Comptes.[53] Eulogies were later pronounced before the Chamber of Peers and the Agricultural Society of the Department of Eure.

The body, placed temporarily in the church, was taken to the village cemetery at Noyers, according to Marbois' express desire. As early as 1832, he had begun correspondence regarding a tomb for himself and his wife.[54] He considered the epitaph and debated whether it should be in French or Latin. Some time before his own death he completed his plans for the monument and raised it above his wife's grave. Since Madame Marbois remained a Protestant, it was not possible to bury her in the village cemetery, which was of course Catholic. Her body was interred just outside the holy ground, the wall removed at this spot, and an obelisk placed between the foot of her grave and the head of the plot reserved for her husband. Scarcely any of the visitors to that quiet village cemetery today sense the tragic romance behind the laconic inscription: *"uxor carissima nata 1764 decissit 1834."* Marbois' own epitaph is a challenge which all men might apply to themselves: *"vita brevis si bene agendo vixit longa nimium si vixit inutilis."*

No fair critic can deny that his life had been well lived. He had set a notable example for material and intellectual achievement. It was his fate to live in an age when revolutions placed the vocations of diplomacy and administration in constant jeopardy. He should not be blamed too severely, therefore, for those occasions on which he appeared more adaptable than courageous. He would have liked to see in his own country the tolerant, liberal spirit he found in America, but he lacked the ardor and self-sacrifice of a crusader. Yet Marbois sensed instinctively the true and permanent interests of the nation. Few have served France so long or so devotedly.

Bibliographical Note

MANUSCRIPTS*

THE ARCHIVES in Paris contain extensive manuscript materials relating to the official career of Barbé-Marbois. The records of his diplomatic service are at the Archives du Ministère des Affaires Étrangères in the series Correspondance Politique and Mémoires et Documents. His years in Germany are covered in *Saxe,* Correspondance Politique, volumes 62–63, and *Bavière,* Correspondance Politique, volumes 159–62. Barbé-Marbois' service in the United States is treated in *États-Unis,* Correspondance Politique, volumes 8–30, and Mémoires et Documents, volumes 4, 7, 8, 14, and 17. The Library of Congress, Manuscripts Division, has photostats of diplomatic documents in the French archives which concern the United States. Papers relating to his mission to the Empire and Austria in 1792 are to be found in *Allemagne,* Correspondance Politique, volumes 120 and 666, and *Autriche,* volume 363. The Louisiana negotiations are recorded in *États-Unis,* Correspondance Politique, volume 55, and *Louisiane et les Florides, Supplément des États-Unis,* volume 8. The most valuable source for the *Négociants Réunis* crisis is *France,* Mémoires et Documents, volume 1415.

The Archives Nationales throw light on most of the phases of Barbé-Marbois' long life. The series *Affaires Étrangères,* B^I 945,

* References to manuscripts in France indicate their location in 1937. Some of these documents may have been lost or destroyed in 1940 when fighting occurred in every important French city connected with Barbé-Marbois' career.

946, contains his consular reports from the United States and much of the correspondence regarding the Longchamps affair. The intendancy in St. Domingue is covered in *Colonies,* B 188, 192, 196, 198, and 199; C⁹ᴬ 156–63; C⁹ᴮ 40, and F³ 59, 72. Evidence on his difficulties in 1793–94 and records of the election to the legislature in 1795 are in AA4 and AA4, C482 (Moselle), respectively. Materials on the deportation to Guiana are to be found in AF* 99, 100, and F⁷ 6156. The papers of his ministry of the public treasury are in AFⁱᵛ 18, 27, 30, 43, 272, 753, 841, 1082, 1084, 1087. The execution of the financial arrangements of the Louisiana cession are treated in AF 1681. Barbé-Marbois' term as minister of justice is dealt with in the series AA5, BB¹⁷ 1, and BB¹⁷ᵃ 1.

Of the French provincial archives only those of the department of Eure at Évreux contribute anything of value. There are the records of Barbé-Marbois' purchases of land, statements of his income, and the records of his participation in the senatorial elections in the department. The archives at Évreux also contain a valuable collection of miscellaneous papers contributed by a M. Regnier. Among these are several items preserved by Antoine Passy, a prefect of the department and a great friend of Barbé-Marbois.

Surprisingly enough the archives of the city of Metz and of the department of Moselle contain little unpublished material on their distinguished son. This may be due to the fact that the city and the village of Buchy, where Barbé-Marbois owned extensive property, were part of Germany from 1871 to 1918. Fortunately, M. Jean Julien Barbé, former archivist of the city, has made a private collection of manuscripts and rare pamphlets on his kinsman.

The most valuable manuscript source is Barbé-Marbois' own memoir written in Guiana, *Notice et dates des changements survenus dans ma situation à différentes époques de ma vie,* now the property of Dr. René Hélot, of Rouen. The memoir carries the author's life only to his deportation, but he has also left some notes on subsequent events with which he originally intended to continue the work. Dr. Hélot has devoted a good deal of time to collecting printed materials and possesses some miscellaneous papers of value.

Bibliographical Note

There are important manuscript sources in American archives and libraries. Both the archives of the Pennsylvania Historical Society and the American Philosophical Society are valuable. The Monroe papers in the New York Public Library tell the story of the origin and composition of the *Histoire de la Louisiane* and also give information on Barbé-Marbois at the end of the Convention and the beginning of the Directory. The Jared Sparks Manuscripts in the Harvard College Library afford further light on the *Histoire de la Louisiane* and provide glimpses of Barbé-Marbois' life in 1828. Correspondence between Barbé-Marbois and distinguished Americans is to be found in the papers of the following in the Manuscripts Division of the Library of Congress: George Washington, Thomas Jefferson, James Madison, James Monroe, Alexander Hamilton, Benjamin Franklin, Robert Morris, and J. Q. Adams. The Papers of the Continental Congress, in the same depot, contain official communications from Barbé-Marbois.

Writings of Barbé-Marbois

BOOKS

Essai sur les moyens d'inspirer aux hommes le gout de la vertu (Paris, 1769).

Socrate en délire, ou Dialogues de Diogène de Synope, by Christopher Martin Wieland. Translated from the German (Dresden and Paris, 1772).

Lettres de Mme la marquise de Pompadour, depuis 1753 jusqu'à 1762 inclusivement. Lettres de Mme la marquise de Pompadour, depuis 1746 jusqu'à 1752 inclusivement. Lettres et réponses écrites à Mme la marquise de Pompadour, depuis 1753 jusqu'à 1762 inclusivement (London, 1772).

La culture du trèfle, de la luzerne et du sainfoin (Metz, 1792).

Réflexions sur la colonie de Saint-Domingue, ou Examen approfondi des causes de sa ruine et des mesures adoptées pour la rétablir (Paris, an IV).

Voyage d'un français aux salines de Bavière et de Salzbourg en 1776 (Paris, an VI).

La richesse des cultivateurs, ou Dialogues entre Benjamin Jachère et Richard Trèfle, laboureurs, sur la culture du trèfle, de la luzerne et du sainfoin. Translated from the German (Paris, 1803).

Mémoire historique relatif aux négotiations qui eurent lieu en 1778 pour la succession de Bavière, by Count Eustach von Goertz. Translated from the German (Paris, 1812).

Complot d'Arnold et de Sir Henry Clinton contre les États-Unis d'Amérique et contre le général Washington, septembre 1780 (Paris, 1816).

De la Guyane, de son état physique, de son agriculture, de son régime intérieur, et du projet de le peupler avec les laboureurs européens (Paris, 1822).

Histoire de la Louisiane et de la cession de cette colonie par la France aux États-Unis de l'Amérique Septentrionale; précédée d'un discours sur la Constitution et le gouvernement des États-Unis (Paris, 1829).

Journal d'un déporté non jugé ou déportation en violation des lois décrétée le 18 fructidor (Brussels, 1835). 2 vols.

Eugene Parker Chase, (ed.), *Our Revolutionary Forefathers* (New York, 1929).

PAMPHLETS AND ADDRESSES

(The Bibliothèque Nationale contains ninety-eight such items, but I have listed here only those works actually used in the preparation of this biography. Unless otherwise indicated references are to the Bibliothèque Nationale collection.)

État des finances de St. Domingue, contenant le résumé des recettes et dépenses de toutes les caisses publiques, depuis le 10 novembre 1785, jusqu'au 1er janvier 1788, par M. Barbé de Marbois, intendant des Isles Françaises sous le vent (Port-au-Prince, 1788).

Réclamation de M. l'intendant de Saint Domingue enregistrée au Conseil Supérieure de cette colonie.

Mémoire et observations du Sieur de Barbé de Marbois, intendant des Isles-sous-le-vent en 1786, 1787, 1788, 1789, sur une dénonciation signée par treize de MM. les députés de Saint-Domingue, et faite á l'Assemblée Nationale au nom d'un des trois comités de la colonie (Paris, 1790).

Observations personnelles à l'intendant de St. Domingue (Paris, 1790).

Mémoire laissé par M. Barbé de Marbois, intendant à St. Domingue à M. l'Ordonnateur, en conformité des ordres du Roi (Port-au-Prince, 26 Octobre, 1789).

Barbé aux citoyens du Conseil Gal de la Commune (Metz, 25 février 1795).

François Barbé aux citoyens de la Commune de Metz (Metz, 1795).

Rapport sur les finances de la Commune de Metz. Fait au Conseil, par le citoyen maire dans la séance du 27 germinal an trois de la République française, une et indivisible.

Le Maire de Metz, destitué, au corps législatif (Paris, 1795). *New York Public Library.*

Dénonciation d'un membre du Conseil des Anciens par fait de trahison (Paris, 1795).

Motion d'ordre pour parvenir à la connoissance de la situation générale de la République. Brumaire an IV.

Opinion du Citoyen Barbé-Marbois sur la marine. 17 pluviôse, an IV.

Rapport fait au Conseil des Anciens, par Barbé-Marbois, au nom de la commission du 28 pluviôse, relative aux ouvrages qui doivent servir de livres élémentaires dans les écoles primaires. Séance du 30 ventôse an IV.

Pecheur, Thiébault et Barbé-Marbois à leurs constituents dans le département de la Moselle. Paris, le 23 floréal an IV (Metz, chez Ch. Lamort).

Rapport fait par Barbé-Marbois sur une résolution qui met des fonds à disposition du ministre des finances. Séance du 28 brumaire an V.

Discours de Barbé-Marbois sur la résolution relative à la retenue sur les matières d'or et d'argent à convertir en espèces. Séance du 16 frimaire an V.

Rapport sur la situation des finances de l'an IV présenté par le Directoire exécutif au Conseil des Anciens. Séances du 28 ventôse et jours suivants.

Discours de Barbé-Marbois sur le message du Directoire exécutif du 14 germinal, concernant la prise de Trieste. Séance du 14 germinal an V.

Discours de Barbé-Marbois sur le message du Directoire exécutif concernant les préliminaires de paix avec l'Autriche. Séance du 11 floréal an V.

Opinion de Barbé-Marbois sur la résolution relative aux salines de la République. Séance du 2 messidor an V.

Opinion de Barbé-Marbois sur la résolution du 7 nivôse concernant les salines de la République. Séance du 8 thermidor an V.

Rapport fait par Barbé-Marbois sur la résolution qui autorise l'envoi d'agens à Saint Domingue. Séance du 5 messidor an V.

Rapport fait par une commission composée des représentants Barbé-Marbois, Bouisson et Chassiron, sur une résolution relative aux dépenses du ministre des relations extérieures. Séance du 16 prairial an V.

Rapport fait par Barbé-Marbois sur l'état des dépenses qui devront être acquittées par le trésor public pendant le cours de l'an VI. Séance du 21 thermidor an V.

Mémoire de Barbé-Marbois adressé à sa femme, Sinamary, le 12 thermidor an VI.

Précis exact de tout ce qui s'est passé à l'inauguration de la statue de Henri IV. Discours prononcé à Sa Majesté. Inauguration de la statue de Henri IV, du 25 août 1818 (Paris, 1818).

Visite des prisons des départements de l'Eure et la Seine Inférieure. Par un membre de la Société Royale pour l'amélioration des prisons (Paris, 1819).

Rapport sur l'état actuel des prisons dans les départements du Calvados, de l'Eure, de la Manche, et de la Seine-Inférieure; et sur la maison de correction de Gaillon. October, 1823 (Paris, 1824).

Observations sur les votes de quarante-un conseils généraux de département concernant la déportation des forçats libérés présentées à Monsieur Le Dauphin par un membre de la Société Royale pour l'amélioration des prisons (Paris, 1828).

Notice sur Barbé-Marbois (Paris, 1836).

Notes

CHAPTER I

1 For this, and other genealogical information, the author is in-indebted to J. J. Barbé, former archivist of the city of Metz, who has established the Barbé family tree.

2 Abbé F. J. Poirier, *Metz, Documents Généalogiques. Armée, noblesse, magistrature, haute bourgeoisie d'après les registres des paroisses 1561–1792* (Paris, 1899), 40.

3 *Notice et dates des changements survenus dans ma situation à différentes époques de ma vie,* an autograph manuscript by Barbé-Marbois now in the possession of Dr. René Hélot, a physician of Rouen, who kindly placed it at the author's disposal. Hereafter this important memoir will be cited as Hélot MS.

4 Émile-Auguste Bégin, *Biographie de la Moselle ou Histoire par ordre alphabétique de toutes les personnes nées dans ce départe-ment qui se sont fait remarquer par leurs actions, leurs talens, leurs écrits, leurs vertus, ou leurs crimes* (Metz, 1831), III, 56. Bégin has left a note in the collection now owned by Jean Julien Barbé stating his belief in the love affair.

5 Hélot MS.

6 Bégin, *Biographie de la Moselle,* III, 57.

7 Hélot MS.

8 Marbois to Vergennes, Dresden, June 19, 1774, Archives du Ministère des Affaires Étrangères, Correspondance Politique, Saxe, Vol. 62, ff. 20–20^v. Hereafter these archives will be cited as AAE.

9 Marbois to Vergennes, Dresden, June 26, 1774, *ibid.*, ff. 25–27^v; Vergennes to Marbois, July 8, 1774, *ibid.*, fol. 37; Marbois to Vergennes, July 24, 1774, *ibid.*, ff. 50–54^v.

10 Hélot MS.

11 Marbois to Vergennes, Dresden, August 24, 1774, AAE Saxe, Vol. 62, ff. 88–91; Marbois to Schröpfer, August 24, 1774, *ibid.*, fol. 96; Marbois to Vergennes, Dresden, September 3, October 16, 1774, *ibid.*, ff. 100–101^v, 137.

12 Marbois to Vergennes, Dresden, July 10, 1774, *ibid.*, fol. 42^v; Vergennes to Marbois, July 23, 1774, *ibid.*, fol. 49.

13 Marbois to Vergennes, Dresden, October 28, 1774, *ibid.*, fol. 153^v; Vergennes to Marbois, November 15, 1774, *ibid.*, fol. 174.

14 *Ibid.*, ff. 107–37^v.

15 Marbois to Vergennes, October 28, 1774, *ibid.*, fol. 152.

16 Reports of November and December, 1774, *ibid.*, ff. 175–96^v.

17 Vergennes to Marbois, February 15, 1775, *ibid.*, ff. 319–20^v.

18 Vergennes to Marbois, March 19, 1775, *ibid.*, ff. 364–66.

19 Vergennes to Marbois, March 23, 1775, *ibid.*, ff. 366–67^v.

20 Vergennes to du Buat, January 31, 1775, *ibid.*, fol. 294; du Buat to Vergennes, Nancy, April 14, 1775, *ibid.*, fol. 412.

21 Marbois to Vergennes, Dresden, April 30, 1775, *ibid.*, ff. 427–28^v.

22 Hélot MS.

23 Marbois to Vergennes, Dresden, January 7, 1776, *ibid.*, Vol. 63, ff. 242–43.

24 *Ibid.*, fol. 252^v.

25 D'Entraignes to Vergennes, Dresden, January 27, 1776, *ibid.*, fol. 283.

26 Hélot MS.

27 Collection Barbé. Under this title will be listed a group of miscellaneous papers brought together by J. J. Barbé.

28 Vergennes to Folard, June 27, July 1, 1776, AAE, Bavière, Vol. 159, ff. 108, 109.

29 Marbois to Vergennes, Munich, July 24, 1776, *ibid.*, fol. 117; Folard to Vergennes, Munich, August 17, 1776, *ibid.*, fol. 147.

30 Vergennes to Marbois, Fontainebleau, November 6, 1776, *ibid.,* fol. 230; Vergennes to Marbois, January 9, 1777, *ibid.,* ff. 10–11.

31 *Ibid.,* Vol. 160, ff. 34–34ᵛ.

32 Luzerne to Vergennes, Munich, March 29, 1777, *ibid.,* fol. 182.

33 Luzerne to Vergennes, Munich, October 10, 1777, *ibid.,* fol. 370.

34 Marbois to Vergennes, Munich, January 17, 22, 24, 1778, *ibid.,* Vol. 161, ff. 76, 88–99, 113.

35 Hélot MS. Many years later Marbois edited and translated Goertz's account of these negotiations—François Barbé-Marbois, *Comte Eustache Goertz, Mémoire historique relatif aux négociations qui eurent lieu en 1778 pour la succession de Bavière* (Paris, 1812).

36 AAE, Bavière, Vol. 162, ff. 77ᵛ–78.

37 To Vergennes, Munich, May 6, 1778, *ibid.,* ff. 113–15ᵛ.

38 To Vergennes, Munich, May 6, 1778, *ibid.,* fol. 118.

39 Hélot MS.

40 Luzerne to Vergennes, Munich, June 20, 1778, AAE, Bavière, Vol. 162, ff. 128–28ᵛ; Vergennes to Luzerne, June 29, 1778, *ibid.,* ff. 235–36.

41 Marbois to Vergennes, July 15, 22, August 8, 1778, *ibid.,* ff. 250–53, 257–60, 266–69ᵛ; Vergennes to Marbois, August 30, *ibid.,* fol. 281.

42 Eugene Parker Chase (ed.), *Our Revolutionary Forefathers* (New York, 1929), 57. Professor Chase has edited and translated the portions of the Hélot MS. relating to Barbé-Marbois' life between 1779 and 1784.

43 Marquis de Marbois, *Notice sur Barbé-Marbois* (Paris, 1836), 3.

44 Parlement de Metz. Copie de l'acte de vente faite par M. F. Vernon de Fortbonnais à F. Barbé de Marbois, la charge de conseiller au Parlement de Metz. Acte du 30 avril 1779. Collection Barbé.

45 Emmanuel Michel, *Biographie du Parlement de Metz* (Metz, 1853).

CHAPTER II

1 Luzerne to Vergennes, June 17, 1779, AAE, États-Unis, Vol. 8.
2 Luzerne to Vergennes, June 16, 1779, *ibid.*
3 Hélot MS. The portions of the Hélot MS. relating to America will be cited in the Chase edition.
4 Chase, *Our Revolutionary Forefathers,* 63.
5 *Ibid.,* introduction, 16.
6 Francis Wharton (ed.), *The Revolutionary Correspondence of the United States* (Washington, 1889), III, 277–78.
7 Marbois to John Adams, Philadelphia, September 29, 1779, *ibid.,* 349.
8 Statement of President Stiles of the Continental Congress, quoted in "Marbois on the Fur Trade," *American Historical Review,* XXIX (1924), 725–26.
9 Luzerne to Vergennes, Boston, August 4, 1779, AAE, États-Unis, Vol. 9, fol. 73; *The Philadelphia Evening Post,* August 16, 1779.
10 Chase, *Our Revolutionary Forefathers,* 65.
11 *Ibid.,* 72, 77–79.
12 *Ibid.,* 87–118.
13 John C. Fitzpatrick (ed.), *The Writings of George Washington* (Washington, 1931——) XVI, 371.
14 Chase, *Our Revolutionay Forefathers,* 119.
15 J. Thomas Scharf and Thompson Wescott, *History of Philadelphia* (Philadelphia, 1884), I, 407.
16 Chase, *Our Revolutionary Forefathers,* 128.
17 Samuel Flagg Bemis, *The Diplomacy of the American Revolution* (New York, 1936), 189.
18 Luzerne to Vergennes, Philadelphia, March 20, 1780, AAE, États-Unis, Vol. 11, fol. 92.
19 Early Proceedings of the American Philosophical Society, January 5, 1781, January 2, March 5, December 9, 1784, October 17, 1788.

20 Two letters to unknown addressees, autumn, 1780, Pennsylvania Historical Society.

21 Chase, *Our Revolutionary Forefathers,* 162.

22 *Ibid.,* 158; Marbois to Washington, April 29, 1780; Washington to Marbois, Morristown, May 5, 1780, Papers of George Washington, Library of Congress.

23 Wharton, *The Revolutionary Correspondence of the United States,* IV, 59; Luzerne to Vergennes, September 17, 1780, AAE, États-Unis, Vol. 13, fol. 190.

24 *Complot d'Arnold et de Sir Henry Clinton contre les États-Unis d'Amérique et contre le général Washington,* septembre 1780 (Paris, 1816).

25 Marbois to Vergennes, October 17, 1780, AAE, États-Unis, Vol. 14, fol. 23; Observations sur les points contestés de la négociation entre l'Espagne et les États-Unis, par de Marbois, chargé d'affaires, *ibid.,* ff.118–34ᵛ; Kathryn Sullivan, *Maryland and France, 1774–1789* (Philadelphia, 1936), 88–90; E. S. Corwin, *French Policy and the American Alliance* (Princeton, 1916), 280–81.

26 Marbois to Vergennes, October 21, 1780, AAE, États-Unis, Vol. 14, fol. 29.

27 Marbois to Vergennes, July 2, 9, 14, 1781, AAE, États-Unis, Vol. 17, 56–59ᵛ, 84, 106; Marbois to Marquis de Castries, minister of the navy and colonies, Archives Nationales, Affaires Étrangères, Bᴵ 945, ff. 110–11ᵛ. Hereafter these archives will be referred to as AN.

28 Marbois to Vergennes, July 5, 1781, *ibid.,* fol. 74.

29 Ellis Paxon Oberholtzer, *Philadelphia, a History of the City and the People* (Philadelphia, n.d.).

30 Marbois to McKain, February 10, 1781, Pennsylvania Historical Society.

31 Albert Ellery Bergh (ed.), *The Writings of Thomas Jefferson* (Washington, 1907), I, 90–91; "Letters of Jefferson to Marbois, 1781, 1783," *American Historical Review,* XII (1906–1907), 75–77.

32 Luzerne to Vergennes, September 28, 1781, AAE, États-Unis,

Vol. 18, fol. 118; Marbois to Vergennes, September 28, 1781, *ibid.,* fol. 347; *ibid.,* Vol. 19, fol. 125; Marbois to Castries, September 28, 1781, AN, Affaires Étrangères, B¹ 945, fol. 127.

33 Marbois to Castries, December 30, 1781, March 17, 1782, AN, Affaires Étrangères, B¹ 945, ff. 169–79, 189–96.

34 Marbois to Castries, November 10, 1781, *ibid.,* ff. 150–59.

35 Marbois to Vergennes, March 13, 1782, AAE, États-Unis, Vol. 20, ff. 407–17. The letter is printed, with extended editorial comment, by Wharton, in *The Revolutionary Correspondence of the United States,* V, 238–41.

36 Luzerne to Vergennes, January 11, 1782, AAE, États-Unis, Vol. 20, fol. 14.

37 W. C. Ford and Gaillard Hunt (eds.), *Journals of the Continental Congress, 1774–89* (Washington, 1914), XXIII, 870.

38 Bemis, *The Diplomacy of the American Revolution,* 220. Many years later Marbois admitted writing the dispatch—Justin Winsor, *Narrative and Critical History of America* (Boston and New York, 1889), VII, 120.

39 Marbois to Castries, December 26, 1782, AN, Affaires Étrangères, B¹ 945, fol. 275.

40 Marbois to Castries, May 20, 1783, *ibid.,* ff. 307–10.

41 Marbois to Castries, July 15, July 24, 1783, *ibid.,* ff. 323–25, fol. 336.

42 Marbois to Castries, July 10, 1783, *ibid.,* ff. 320–22ᵛ.

43 Marbois to Castries, July 24, 1783, *ibid.,* ff. 342ᵛ–43.

44 Marbois to Castries, August 26, 1783, *ibid.,* ff. 366–69.

45 F. L. Nussbaum, "The French Colonial Arrêt of 1784," *South Atlantic Quarterly,* XXVII (1928) 62–78.

46 Marbois to Governor [Dickinson], Annapolis, January 2, 1784, Pennsylvania Historical Society; Marbois to Castries, Annapolis, January 10, 1784, AN, Affaires Étrangères, B¹ 946, ff. 3–4.

47 F. P. Blair (ed.), *The Diplomatic Correspondence of the United States of America from September 10, 1783 to March 4, 1789* (Washington, 1833), I, 79.

CHAPTER III

1 Marbois to Vergennes, June 10, 1783, AAE, États-Unis, Vol. 24, ff. 315–16ᵛ; Luzerne to Vergennes, June 10, 1783, *ibid.,* fol. 185.

2 Copy of the marriage contract, Archives de l'Eure, Évreux; Marbois to Castries, June 18, 1784, AN, Affaires Étrangères, Bᴵ 946, fol. 51.

3 Mount Vernon, June 20, 1784, Jared Sparks (ed.), *Writings of George Washington* (Boston, 1839–40), IX, 50–51. Marbois had announced the forthcoming marriage to Washington on June 8. Papers of George Washington, Library of Congress.

4 Luzerne to Vergennes, June 18, 1783, AAE, États-Unis, Vol. 24, fol. 206.

5 Edmund C. Burnett (ed.), *Letters of the Members of the Continental Congress* (Washington, 1921–36), VII, 484.

6 Wharton, *The Revolutionary Correspondence of the United States,* V, 806; Blair, *The Diplomatic Correspondence of the United States* I, 103–104.

7 Luzerne to Vergennes, Philadelphia, June 19, 1784, AN, Affaires Étrangères, Bᴵ 946, ff. 41–47.

8 Marbois to the President of the Executive Council of Pennsylvania, May 17, 1784, Archives of the Pennsylvania Historical Society.

9 Déposition de Manuel Josephson (an eye witness), AN, Affaires Etrangères, Bᴵ 946, fol. 60.

10 *Ibid.,* fol. 62.

11 Luzerne to President of the Executive Council of Pennsylvania, May 19, 1784, *ibid.,* fol. 88.

12 Luzerne to Vergennes, June 19, 1784, *ibid.,* ff. 41–47.

13 Dickinson to Luzerne, May 20, 21, 22, 25, 26, 27, 1784, Archives of the Pennsylvania Historical Society.

14 Dickinson to Marbois, May 27, 1784, *ibid.*

15 Marbois to Luzerne, Chester, 2:30, May 24, 1784, *ibid.*

16 Dickinson to Luzerne, June 4, 1784, AN, Affaires Étrangères, Bᴵ 946, fol. 91; ff. 111–11ᵛ.

17 Dickinson to Luzerne, June 11, 1784, Archives of the Pennsylvania Historical Society; *The Freeman's Journal*, Philadelphia, June 9, 1784.

18 Blair, *The Diplomatic Correspondence of the United States*, I, 123–25.

19 Ford and Hunt, *Journals of the Continental Congress, 1774–89*, XXVIII, 564–65.

20 Luzerne to Marbois, June 20, 1784, AAE, États-Unis, Vol. 27, ff. 432–33.

21 Correspondance entre Wm. Bradford, Procureur Général de Pennsylvanie, et de Marbois, Consul Général, au sujet de l'affaire de Longchamps. Juin 24–25, 1784, *ibid.*, ff. 443–46^v.

22 Marbois to Vergennes, August 14, October 8, 1784, Vol. 28, ff. 136–39, ff. 306–10.

23 Enclosed by Marbois in his letter of July 1, 1784, to Castries, AN, Affaires Étrangères, B^I 946, ff. 133–37. "An Independent Patriot" published a similar plea in *The Freeman's Journal*, June 30, 1784, and the paper defended Longchamps in its issues of July 28, August 4, 11, and 18.

24 Marbois to Castries, November 9, 1784, AN, Affaires Étrangères, B^I 946, ff. 169–72; Marbois to Vergennes, November 10, 1784, AAE, États-Unis, Vol. 28, ff. 366–69.

25 Vergennes to Marbois, October 12, 1784, *ibid.*, Vol. 28, ff. 319–20. On November 9, Marbois thanked Castries for a letter of August 8 expressing sympathy for the insult.—AN, Affaires Étrangères, B^I 946, ff. 169–72.

26 Marbois to Vergennes, November 10, 1784, AAE, États-Unis, Vol. 28, ff. 366–69.

27 Marbois to M. de Cabres (an official in the ministry of the navy and colonies), January 6, 1784, AN, Affaires Étrangères, B^I 946, ff. 190–91^v.

28 Élise Moore de Marbois to Marie Antoinette, *ibid.*, ff. 192–93^v.

29 Blair, *The Diplomatic Correspondence of the United States*, I, 153, 155.

30 *Ibid.*, 157–60.

31 Ford and Hunt, *Journals of the Continental Congress,* XXVIII, 314–15.

32 Vergennes to Marbois, Versailles, February 8, 1785, AAE, États-Unis. Vol. 29, ff. 43–44ᵛ.

33 Blair, *The Diplomatic Correspondence of the United States,* I, 231–32; Ford and Hunt, *Journals of the Continental Congress,* XXVIII, 314–15.

34 American sources on the episode are utilized in an article by Alfred Rosenthal, "The Marbois-Longchamps Affair," *Pennsylvania Magazine of History and Biography,* July, 1939, pp. 295–301.

35 Extrait du journal d'un voyage chez les sauvages Oneidas, Tuscaroras, etc., par Barbé-Marbois, AAE, États-Unis, Vol. 28, ff. 204–38. This journal has been translated by Chase in his *Our Revolutionary Forefathers.* It is the basis for Vicomte de Montbas' *Avec Lafayette chez les Iroquois* (Paris, 1929). Marbois to Vergennes, à la Bourgade des Oneidas, September 30, 1784, AAE, États-Unis, Vol. 28, ff. 266–71; Marbois to Vergennes, Albany, October 9, 1784, *ibid.,* ff. 311–14.

36 Mémoire sur le commerce des fourrures avec les sauvages de la Rivière du Nord. September 30, 1784, *ibid.,* ff. 272–86. This memoir has been translated, "Marbois on the Fur Trade," *American Historical Review,* XXIX, 726–40.

37 Marbois to Vergennes, Trenton, October 30, 1784, AAE, États-Unis, Vol. 28, ff. 335–37.

38 To Congress, November 19, 1784, Blair, *The Diplomatic Correspondence of the United States,* I, 134–35.

39 Marbois to Vergennes, Philadelphia, November 20, 1784, AAE, États-Unis, Vol. 28, ff. 397–401ᵛ.

40 Marbois to Vergennes, Philadelphia, December 26, 1784, *ibid.,* ff. 461–66.

41 Marbois to Jay, Trenton, December 24, 1784, Blair, *The Diplomatic Correspondence of the United States,* I, 146; committee report of Congress, February 11, 1785, Ford and Hunt, *Journals of the Continental Congress,* XXIII, 57; Jay to Robert Mor-

ris, New York, March 31, 1785, Blair, *The Diplomatic Correspondence of the United States,* I, 184; Morris to Marbois, Philadelphia, April 15, 1785, *ibid.,* 185; Marbois to Morris, Philadelphia, April 15, 1785, *ibid.,* 186; Morris to Marbois, April 16, 1785, *ibid.,* 188; Morris to Jay, Philadelphia, April 16, 1785, *ibid.,* 191; Jay to Morris, New York, April 22, 1785, *ibid.,* 192.

42 Charles Warren, "What Has Become of the Portraits of Louis XVI and Marie Antoinette Belonging to Congress?" Massachusetts Historical Society, *Proceedings, LIX,* 45–85.

43 Marbois to Jay, New York, February 22, 1785, Blair, *The Diplomatic Correspondence of the United States,* I, 161–62; Marbois to Vergennes, Philadelphia, March 16, 1785, AAE, États-Unis, Vol. 29, ff. 107–107^v.

44 Marbois to an unknown addressee, Philadelphia, January 8, 1785; Marbois to John Dickinson, January 14, 1785; Marbois to an unknown addressee, Philadelphia, March 17, 1785, Archives of the Pennsylvania Historical Society.

45 Marbois to Castries, AN, Affaires Étrangères, B^I 946, ff. 216–19^v.

46 Marbois to Jay, May 19, 1785, Blair, *The Diplomatic Correspondence of the United States,* I, 200.

47 Castries to Vergennes, June 10, 1785, AAE, États-Unis, Vol. 30, fol. 41; Vergennes to Castries, June 12, 1785, *ibid.,* fol. 45.

48 Vergennes to Marbois, June 20, 1785, *ibid.,* Vol. 30, ff. 57–57^v.

49 Hélot MS.

50 Marbois to George Washington, September 14, 1785, Papers of George Washington, Manuscripts Division, Library of Congress.

51 Otto to Vergennes, New York, August 26, 1785, AAE, États-Unis, Vol. 30, ff. 246–48.

52 Marbois to Vergennes, New York, September 16, 1785, *ibid.,* ff. 300–301.

53 *Ibid.,* fol. 230.

54 Jay to Marbois, September 12, 1785, *ibid.,* ff. 294–95; Otto to Vergennes, New York, September 28, 1785, *ibid.,* ff. 317–19.

55 *Ibid.*

56 Mount Vernon, September 25, 1785, Sparks, *Writings of Washington,* IX, 130.

57 To Marbois, New York, September, 1785, Blair, *The Diplomatic Correspondence of the United States,* I, 250.

58 To Jay, New York, September 24, 1785, *ibid.,* I, 251.

CHAPTER IV

1 Mémoire du Roi pour servir d'instructions au S. M^{qis}. Du Chilleau M^{al}. des Camps et armées de S. M.^{te} G^{eur} de St. Domingue et au S^{r}. Marbé [*sic*] de Marbois Intend^{t}. de la même colonie 1er août 1788, AN, Col. F^{3} 72, ff. 231–46.

2 Marbois to the minister of the navy and colonies, Le Cap, October 23, 1785, *ibid.,* Col. C^{9A} 156.

3 Mémoire du Roi pour servir d'instructions au S^{r}. Comte de La Luzerne Lieutenant Général des armées de Sa Majesté Gouverneur de St. Domingue et au S^{r}. Barbé de Marbois, Intendant de la même colonie, 6 X^{bre} 1785, *ibid.,* ff. 203–10.

4 *Ibid.,* Col. B 196.

5 To Castries, Les Cayes, January 5, 1786, *ibid.,* C^{9A} 157.

6 Castries to Marbois, Fontainebleau, October 26, 1785, *ibid.,* Col. B 188.

7 Castries to Marbois, Versailles, March 23, 1786, *ibid.,* Col. B 192.

8 To Castries, February 2, 1786, *ibid.,* Col. C^{9A} 157; Castries to Luzerne and Marbois, May 12, 1786, *ibid.,* Col. B 192, ff. 115–16.

9 Hélot MS.

10 AN, Col. B 192, fol. 159.

11 *Ibid.,* ff. 174–75.

12 *Ibid.,* fol. 227.

13 Minister to Marbois, July 20, November 9, 1786, *ibid.,* ff. 150, 229.

14 To Castries, May 23, 1786, *ibid.,* Col. C^{9A} 157.

15 To Castries, August, 1786, *ibid.,* Col. C^{9A} 158.

16 *Ibid.,* Col. C^{9A} 160.

17 Marbois to Luzerne, then minister of the navy and colonies, September 4, December 5, 1788, *ibid.,* Col. C⁹ᴬ 161.

18 Luzerne to Vincent, then the governor, and Marbois, October 9, 1788, *ibid.,* Col. B 198, fol. 168.

19 Vincent and Marbois to Luzerne, June 25, 1789, *ibid.,* Col. C⁹ᴬ 162.

20 Ministerial circular to all colonial governors and intendants, Versailles, September 22, 1786, *ibid.,* ff. 188–88ᵛ.

21 To Luzerne and Marbois, Versailles, December 27, 1786, *ibid.,* ff. 260–61.

22 Versailles, February 16, 1787, *ibid.,* Col. B 196, fol. 52–52ᵛ; to Luzerne, August 28, 1787, *ibid.,* ff. 178–78ᵛ; to Marbois, August 28, 1787, *ibid.,* ff. 178ᵛ–79.

23 Hélot MS.

24 Luzerne and Marbois to Castries, September 9, 1787, AN, Col. C⁹ᴬ 158.

25 Luzerne and Marbois to Castries, August 29, 1787, *ibid.,* Col. C⁹ᴬ 158; Luzerne to Vincent and Marbois, January 3, 1788, *ibid.,* Col. B 198, fol. 1.

26 *Ibid.,* C⁹ᴬ 159–60.

27 *État des finances de St. Domingue, contenant le résumé des recettes et dépenses de toutes les caisses publiques, depuis le 10 novembre 1785, jusqu'au 1er janvier 1788.* Par M. Barbé de Marbois, Intendant des Isles Françaises sous le vent (Port-au-Prince, 1788).

28 AN, Col. B 198, fol. 72ᵛ.

29 *Ibid.,* Col. C⁹ᴬ 163.

30 Archives de la ville de Metz, 1059. She was born in Philadelphia on August 21, 1788, and a record of her baptism is inscribed in the register of the parish of St. Simplice, Metz.

31 Marbois to Luzerne, April 2, 1789, AN, Col. C⁹ᴬ 163.

32 *Correspondance de M. le Marquis du Chilleau, gouverneur général de St. Domingue, avec M. le Comte de la Luzerne, ministre de la marine & M. de Marbois, intendant de St. Domingue, relativement à l'introduction des farines étrangères dans cette*

colonie; remise à Mm. les députés de St. Domingue après la demande de M. le président de l'Assemblée Nationale en date du 16 septembre 1789.

33 *Réclamation de M. l'intendant de Saint Domingue enregistrée au Conseil Supérieur de cette colonie.*

34 Marbois to Luzerne, May 11, 1789, AN, Col. C^{9A} 163.

35 Marbois to Luzerne, May 29, 1789, *ibid.*

36 To Luzerne, *ibid.*

37 Memoir presented to Louis XVI, approved May 22, 1789, *ibid.,* Col. C^{9B} 40.

38 Luzerne to Marbois, May 31, 1789, *ibid.,* Col. B 199, fol. 92.

39 Decree of July 3, 1789, *ibid.,* Col. C^{9B} 40.

40 Luzerne to Chilleau, September 12, 1789, *ibid.,* Col. C^{9A} 163.

41 Barbé-Marbois, *Journal d'un déporté non jugé ou déportation en violation des lois décrétée le 18 fructidor* [September 4, 1797] (Brussels, 1835), II, 265.

42 Peinier to Luzerne, August 22, 1789; Marbois to Luzerne, August 19, 1789, AN, Col C^{9A} 163.

43 Versailles, November 6, 1788. *ibid.,* Col. B 198, ff. 180–81.

44 Vincent and Marbois to Luzerne, December 5, 1788, December 8, 1788, *ibid.,* Col. C^{9A} 161.

45 *Mémoire et observations du Sieur Barbé de Marbois, intendant des Isles-sous-le-vent en 1786, 1787, 1788, 1789, sur une dénonciation signée par treize de MM. les députés de Saint-Domingue, et faite à l'Assemblée Nationale au nom d'un des trois comités de la colonie* (Paris, 1790), 14–16.

46 Memoir of June 29, 1789, AN, Col. C^{9B} 40.

47 *Ibid.,* Col. C^{9B} 40.

48 *Ibid.,* Col B 199, ff. 135–36^{v}.

49 *Ibid.,* Col. B 199, ff. 148–48^{v}.

50 Peinier and Marbois to Luzerne, *Ibid.,* Col. C^{9B} 40.

51 Peinier and Marbois to Luzerne, October 10, 1789, *ibid.*

52 *Arrêt de l'Assemblée Provinciale de la Partie du Nord de Saint Domingue séant au Cap, contre Barbé de Marbois, ses conseils, complices et adhérens,* 1789.

53 To Luzerne, October 17, 1789, AN, Col. C^{9A} 162.

54 Barbé-Marbois, *Observations personnelles à l'intendant de St. Domingue* (Paris, 1790), 16.

55 Barbé-Marbois, *Mémoire laissé par M. Barbé de Marbois, intendant à St. Domingue à M. l'Ordonnateur, en conformité des ordres du roi,* Port-au-Prince, 26 Octobre 1789.

56 AN, Col. F^3 59, ff. 77.

57 Peinier to Luzerne, November 12, 1789, *ibid.,* Col. C^{9A} 163.

58 Barbé-Marbois, *Observations personnelles,* 20.

59 Peinier to Luzerne, October 27, 1789, AN, Col. C^{9A} 163.

60 A. de Laujon, *Souvenirs de trente années de voyages à St. Domingue, dans plusieurs colonies étrangères, et au continent d'Amérique* (Paris, 1835), I, 283–85.

61 Barbé-Marbois, *Observations personnelles,* 20.

62 Marbois to Luzerne, Cadiz, December 3, 1789, *ibid., Gazette Nationale ou le Moniteur Universel,* I, (December 27, 1789), 481.

63 *Mémoire et observations du Sieur Barbé de Marbois.*

64 Marbois to the President of the National Assembly, July 12, 1790, *Gazette Nationale ou le Moniteur Universel,* V, (July 18, 1790), 155–56.

65 A letter signed "Barbé, ci-devant de Marbois" (August 17, 1790), *ibid.,* V, 412; letter from "Barbé, dit Marbois" (February 5, 1791), *ibid.,* VII, 297.

CHAPTER V

1 Hélot MS.

2 M. Viville, *Dictionnaire du département de la Moselle,* an 1817.

3 *Statistique historique, industrielle et commerciale du département de la Moselle* (Metz, 1844).

4 In 1937 the house belonged to M. Jean Bidon, who purchased the estate and moved there after the World War, when the territory was returned to France by Germany.

5 *La culture du trèfle, de la luzerne et du sainfoin* (Metz, 1792).

6 Hélot MS.

7 Instruction pour le Ministre du Roi auprès de la Diète Germanique, 1er Janvier 1792, AAE, Allemagne, Vol. 120, ff. 176–181^v; also printed in Bertrand Auerbach, *Recueil des instructions données aux ambassadeurs et ministres de France* (Paris, 1912), 375–81. His official correspondence was conducted under the name of de Marbois, although in Metz he was known as Barbé. Both names are employed in this chapter, the choice depending upon the subject being discussed.

8 Before becoming Emperor in 1790, Leopold had been the Grand Duke of Tuscany.

9 Hélot MS.

10 Then the capital of the Austrian Netherlands, which the Hapsburgs had ruled since 1713.

11 *Gazette Nationale ou le Moniteur Universel,* XI, (January 25, 1792), 201.

12 Hélot MS.

13 De Lessart to Noailles, January 23, 1792, AAE, Autriche, Vol. 363, ff. 102–102^v.

14 Hélot MS.

15 Noailles to De Lessart, February 1, 11, 14, 1792, AAE, Autriche, Vol. 363, fol. 121^v ff.

16 Marbois to De Lessart, Ratisbon, March 17, 1792, *ibid.,* Allemagne, Vol. 666, ff. 57–61.

17 De Lessart to Marbois, March 9, 1792, *ibid.,* ff. 38–42^v; De Lessart to Noailles, March 9, 1792, *ibid.,* Autriche, Vol. 363, ff. 216–17.

18 Marbois to De Lessart, Ratisbon, March 17, 1792, *ibid.,* Allemagne, Vol. 666, ff. 56–56^v.

19 Dumouriez to Marbois, April 1, 1792, *ibid.,* fol. 82.

20 Hélot MS.

21 Dumouriez to Marbois, April 11, 1792, AAE, Allemagne, Vol. 666, ff. 90–90^v.

22 Bégin, *Biographie de la Moselle,* III, 63.

23 René Paquet, *Bibliographie analytique de l'histoire de Metz pendant la révolution, 1789–1800* (Paris, 1926), 301, 674–75.

24 Morris to Lebrun, March 23, 1793; Morris to Madame de Marbois, March 23; Morris to Madame de Marbois, April 1; Lebrun to Morris, March 27; Morris to Madame de Marbois, April 26; Morris to Madame de Marbois, June 9; Morris to Deforgues, August 9; Deforgues to Morris, August 15, 1793; Deforgues to Morris, August 20; Morris to Madame de Marbois, October 10; Morris to Madame de Marbois, January 20, 1794; Morris to Madame de Marbois, March 24, 1794; Morris to Madame de Marbois, July 25, 1794. Copies of these letters, taken from the Morris papers in the Library of Congress, were given the author by Miss Beatrix Davenport and are here cited with her kind permission.

25 Paquet, *Bibliographie analytique de l'histoire de Metz pendant la révolution,* 305.

26 Pétition de François Barbé ancien Intendant de St. Domingue, tendante à faire cesser l'arrestation provisoirement prononcée contre lui d'après le Décret du 1er pluviôse [January 20, 1794]. Aux citoyens composant le comité de surveillance du District de Morhange, à Buchy le 10 pluviôse [January 29, 1794] l'an deux de la République, AN, AA⁴, Pièce 285.

27 Barbé-Marbois, *Journal d'un déporté,* 14.

28 Paquet, *Bibliographie analytique de l'histoire de Metz pendant la révolution,* 336; Jean Julien Barbé, *Les municipalités de Metz* (Metz, 1922).

29 *François Barbé aux citoyens de la Commune de Metz* (Metz, chez Antoine, Imprimeur, 1795).

30 *Barbé aux citoyens du Conseil Gal de la Commune* (Metz, February 25, 1795), Collection Bégin.

31 Paquet, *Bibliographie analytique de l'histoire de Metz pendant la révolution,* 277–81.

32 *Ibid.,* 1323–24.

33 *Ibid.,* 498.

34 Hélot MS.

35 Extrait du registre des délibérations du Conseil Général de la Commune de Metz, April 16, 1795, Paquet, *Bibliographie analytique de l'histoire de Metz pendant la révolution,* 1325.

36 *Ibid.,* 1326.

37 Mayor and Council to Lepayen, *ibid.,* 1326–27.

38 *Ibid.,* 1327.

39 *Rapport sur les finances de la Commune de Metz.* Fait au Conseil, par le citoyen maire dans la séance du 27 germinal [April 16, 1795] an trois de la République française, une et indivisible. This report was printed at the personal expense of the mayor and councilors and distributed to the citizens of the city.

40 Paquet, *Bibliographie analytique de l'histoire de Metz pendant la révolution,* 338.

41 Barbé to Monroe, Metz, September 28, 1795, Monroe Papers, New York Public Library.

42 Barbé-Marbois, *Le Maire de Metz, destitué, au corps législatif* (Paris, 1795), 10, New York Public Library.

43 AN, C 482 (Moselle).

44 Barbé-Marbois, *Dénonciation d'un membre du Conseil des Anciens par fait de trahison* (Paris, November 6, 1795), 9–12, New York Public Library.

45 *Journal du Matin,* October 25, 1795, in Paquet, *Bibliographie analytique de l'histoire de Metz pendant la révolution,* 384. The article was reprinted by "une société des patriotes de Metz."

46 *Gazette Nationale ou le Moniteur Universel,* XXVI, (November 11, 15, 1795), 398–99.

CHAPTER VI

1 A. Meynier, *Les coups d'état du Directoire* (Paris, 1927–28), I, 5–6; Louis Madelin, *The French Revolution* (London, 1916), 488.

2 *Opinions, rapports et choix d'écrits politiques de Charles-François Lebrun, Duc de Plaisance, recueillis et mis en ordre par son fils ainé, et précédés d'une notice biographique* (Paris, 1829), 68.

3 Louis Adolphe Thiers, *The History of the French Revolution* (London, 1881), IV, 346.

4 *The French Revolution,* 488.

5 G. Pariset, "La révolution, 1792–99," in *Histoire de France contemporaine* (Paris, 1920), II, 296.

6 Thiers, *The History of the French Revolution,* IV, 347; Barbé-Marbois, *Journal d'un déporté,* 17–19.

7 *Ibid.,* I, 38.

8 *Gazette Nationale ou le Moniteur Universel,* XXVI (November 22, 1795), 483–84.

9 *Ibid.* (November 23, 1795), 494–95: *Motion d'ordre pour parvenir à la connoissance de la situation générale de la République,* par Barbé-Marbois, Député du département de la Moselle (Paris, brumaire an IV), Bibliothèque Nationale.

10 *Gazette Nationale ou le Moniteur Universel* (November 26, 1795).

11 *Opinion du Citoyen Barbé-Marbois sur la marine.* Séance du 7 pluviôse l'an IVᵉ de la République [January 27, 1796].

12 *Rapport fait au Conseil des Anciens, par Barbé-Marbois, au nom de la commission du 28 pluviôse, relative aux ouvrages qui doivent servir de livres élémentaires dans les écoles primaires.* Séance du 30 ventôse an IV [March 20, 1796]. Bibliothèque Nationale.

13 *Pecheur, Thiébault et Barbé-Marbois à leurs constituents dans le département de la Moselle,* Paris le 23 floréal an IV [May 12, 1796] (Metz, chez Ch. Lamort, imprimeur). Bibliothèque Nationale.

14 George Duruy (ed.), *Memoirs of Barras* (New York, 1895–96), II, 244.

15 *Ibid.,* 375.

16 *Ibid.,* 493.

17 *Ibid.,* 583.

18 *Rapport fait par Barbé-Marbois sur une résolution qui met des fonds à disposition du ministre des finances.* Séance du 28 brumaire an V [November 18, 1796]. Bibliothèque Nationale.

19 *Discours de Barbé-Marbois sur la résolution relative à la retenue sur les matières d'or et d'argent à convertir en espèces.* Séance du 16 frimaire an V [December 6, 1796]. Bibliothèque Nationale.

20 *Rapport sur la situation des finances de l'an IV présentée par le Directoire exécutif au Conseil des Anciens.* Séances du 28 ventôse et jours suivants. Barbé-Marbois, rapporteur. Bibliothèque Nationale.

21 *Discours de Barbé-Marbois sur le message du Directoire exécutif du 14 germinal, concernant la prise de Trieste.* Séance du 14 germinal an V [April 3, 1797]. Bibliothèque Nationale.

22 *Discours de Barbé-Marbois sur le message du Directoire exécutif concernant les préliminaires de paix avec l'Autriche.* Séance du 11 floréal an V [April 30, 1797]. Bibliothèque Nationale.

23 A. Mathiez, *Le Directoire* (Paris, 1934), 287.

24 "The French Revolution," *Cambridge Modern History* (Cambridge, 1904), VIII, 507.

25 Madelin, *Les coups d'état du Directoire*, 524; F. A. Aulard, *The French Revolution*, London, 1910), IV, 54.

26 Barbé-Marbois, *Journal d'un déporté*, I, 57–58.

27 *Ibid.*, I, 54.

28 *Ibid.*, I, 62.

29 Aulard, *The French Revolution*, IV, 54.

30 Augustin Challamel, *Les clubs contre-révolutionnaires* (Paris, 1895), 513.

31 *Opinion de Barbé-Marbois sur la résolution relative aux salines de la République.* Séance du 2 messidor an V [June 20, 1797]. Bibliothèque Nationale. *Opinion de Barbé-Marbois sur la résolution du 7 nivôse concernant les salines de la République.* Séance du 8 thermidor an V [July 26, 1797]. Bibliothèque Nationale.

32 *Rapport fait par Barbé-Marbois sur la résolution qui autorise l'envoi d'agens à Saint Domingue.* Séance du 5 messidor an V [June 23, 1797]. Bibliothèque Nationale.

33 *Rapport fait par une commission composée des représentants Barbé-Marbois, Bouisson et Chassiron, sur une résolution relative aux dépenses du ministre des relations extérieures.* Rapporteur Barbé-Marbois. Séance du 16 prairial an V [June 4, 1797]. Bibliothèque Nationale.

34 "Note du rapporteur," *ibid.*, 33–34.

35 Barbé-Marbois, *Journal d'un déporté*, I, 22.

36 *Rapport fait par Barbé-Marbois sur l'état des dépenses qui devront être acquittées par le trésor public pendant le cours de l'an VI.* Séance du 21 thermidor an V [August 8, 1797]. Bibliothèque Nationale.

37 Madelin, *The French Revolution*, 532.

38 *Ibid.*, 524.

39 Barbé-Marbois, *Journal d'un déporté*, I, 61, 64.

40 *Ibid.*, I, 23.

41 *Ibid.*, I, 25.

42 *Ibid.*, I, 70.

43 *Ibid.*, I, 72–74.

44 *Ibid.*, I, 79.

45 *Mémoire de Barbé-Marbois adressé à sa femme,* Sinamary, le 12 thermidor an VI [July 30, 1798]. Bibliothèque Nationale.

46 Barbé-Marbois, *Journal d'un déporté*, I, 124–26.

47 Barbé-Marbois à la Citoyenne Lafon-Ladebat ou à la Citoyenne Lavoisier pour remettre à sa femme, 23 fructidor [September 9], note from a book catalogue, Archives du département de l'Eure, Évreux.

48 Barbé-Marbois, *Journal d'un déporté*, I, 138–42; Thiers, *The History of the French Revolution*, V, 179.

49 Barbé-Marbois, *Journal d'un déporté*, I, 158.

50 *Ibid.*, I, 175–95, 278.

51 *Ibid.*, II, 116, 215–51.

52 *Ibid.*, I, 203.

53 *Ibid.*, II, 255–65.

54 *Ibid.*, II, 71–72; Frédéric Masson (ed.), *Journal de ma déportation à la Guyane française par Laffon-Ladebat* (Paris, 1912), 43.

55 J. D. Freytag, *Mémoires* (Paris, 1824), 2 vols. Freytag was the commander in Guiana.

56 Barbé-Marbois *Journal d'un déporté*, II, 190–94.

57 *Ibid.*, II, 268–77.

58 Documents in Paquet, *Bibliographie analytique de l'histoire de*

Metz pendant la révolution, 674–75; AN, AF* 99, Register for November 22, 1798.

59 AN, F⁷ 6156, plaq 6, Police Générale, Affaires Politiques, July 5, 1798.
60 Barbé-Marbois, *Journal d'un déporté,* I, 185.
61 *Ibid.,* AF* 100, Register for January 10, 1799.
62 *Ibid.,* Register for February 20, 1799.
63 *Ibid.,* AFⁱⁱⁱ* 102, Register for June 10, 1799.
64 Barbé-Marbois, *Journal d'un déporté,* II, 206–20.
65 *Ibid.,* II, 23.
66 *Ibid.,* II, 220–25.
67 *Ibid.,* II, 227.
68 *Ibid.,* II, 226.

CHAPTER VII

1 F. A. Aulard, *Paris sous le consulat* (Paris, 1904–1909), I, 180.
2 Hélot MS. The narrative of Barbé-Marbois' memoirs stops with his deportation, but he left a valuable group of notes on his relations with Napoleon. These notes were written immediately following the interviews and were designed to form a basis for a continuation of the author's memoirs.
3 Decree of First Consul, AN, AFⁱᵛ 18, plaq 96.
4 Decree of December 14, 1800, AN, AFⁱᵛ 27, plaq 149.
5 Barbé-Marbois au Premier Consul, au Port Brieux, January 10, 1801, *ibid.*
6 AN, AFⁱᵛ 30, plaq 172, 173.
7 *Ibid.,* AFⁱᵛ 43, plaq 242.
8 Jared Sparks, *The Life of Gouverneur Morris with Selections from His Correspondence and Miscellaneous Papers* (Boston, 1832), III, 156.
9 Barbé-Marbois to Napoleon, August 7, 1801, AN, AFⁱᵛ 1087.
10 Hélot MS.
11 *Ibid.*
12 *Ibid.*

13 AN, AF^iv 1082, dossier 4; *ibid., AF^iv* 1087.

14 To Napoleon, December 27, 1802, *ibid.*

15 Harold C. Deutch, *The Genesis of Napoleonic Imperialism* (Cambridge, 1938), presents the latest scholarly study of international relations at this time. He places the major responsibility for the rupture of the Treaty of Amiens upon Great Britain.

16 For an extended account of the negotiations, see E. Wilson Lyon, *Louisiana in French Diplomacy, 1759–1804* (Norman, 1934).

17 The preparation of the volume is explained in E. Wilson Lyon, "Barbé-Marbois and His *Histoire de la Louisiane,* Correspondence with James Monroe," *Franco-American Review,* I (1937), 357–67.

18 Barbé-Marbois, *Histoire de la Louisiane et de la cession de cette colonie par la France aux États-Unis de l'Amérique Septentrionale; précédée d'un discours sur la Constitution et le gouvernement des États-Unis* (Paris, 1829), 286–87.

19 *Ibid.,* 298–99.

20 Livingston to Madison, April 11, 1803, *Annals of Congress 1802–1803* (Washington, 1851), 1126–28.

21 Livingston to Madison, April 13, 1803, *ibid., 1128–32.*

22 Monroe to Lafayette, May 2, 1829, MS. The Pierpont Morgan Library, New York.

23 Barbé-Marbois, *Histoire de la Louisiane,* 299.

24 Livingston to Madison, April 17, 1803, *Annals of Congress 1802–1803,* 1132–33.

25 Barbé-Marbois to Talleyrand, April 21, 1803, AAE, États-Unis, Vol. 55.

26 *Correspondance de Napoléon 1er,* VIII (Paris, 1861), 365.

27 To Napoleon, July 30, 1803, AN, AF^iv 1087.

28 London, February 14, 1804, Hamilton, *Writings of Monroe,* IV, 140–43.

29 Barbé-Marbois to Talleyrand, AAE, *Louisiane et les Florides,* VIII.

30 Napoleon to Barbé-Marbois, St. Cloud, May 21, 1803. *Correspondance de Napoléon 1er,* VIII, 404.

31 Barbé-Marbois to Napoleon, September 11, 1804, AN, AF[iv] 1087.
32 Barbé-Marbois to Napoleon, Brussels, July 13, 1803, AN AF[iv] 1084.
33 Barbé-Marbois to Napoleon, July 20, 1803, *ibid.*
34 Hélot MS.
35 November 2, 1803, *ibid.*
36 November 27, December 9, 1803, *ibid.*
37 March 20, 21; April 20, 1804, *ibid.*
38 General Fleichmann (ed.), *Memoirs of Miot de Melito* (New York, 1881), 311.
39 Barbé-Marbois to Napoleon, March 19, 1804, AN, AF[iv] 1087.
40 Hélot MS., April, May 16, December 2, 1804.
41 Acquisitions de Barbé-Marbois, Archives du département de l'Eure, Évreux.
42 Élections de l'an XI. Liste des candidats présentés pour le Sénat Conservateur par le collège électoral du département de l'Eure. Archives de l'Eure, Évreux.
43 Correspondance générale sur les opérations électorales an XII, *ibid.*
44 Procès Verbaux du collège électoral de département du département de l'Eure. Session du Vingt Thermidor, an XII, *ibid.*
45 Session de 21 thermidor (August 9), *ibid.*
46 Barbé-Marbois to Napoleon, Évreux, August 10, 1804, AN, AF[iv] 1087.
47 Barbé-Marbois to Napoleon, August 12, 1804 (marked "Pour Votre Majesté Seule"), *ibid.,* AF[iv] 1082.
48 Barbé-Marbois to Napoleon, August 12, 30, September 23, December 8, 1804; February 25, April 2, 1805, *ibid.*
49 Barbé-Marbois to Napoleon, May 6, 1805, *ibid.,* AF[iv] 1087.
50 Barbé-Marbois to Napoleon, *ibid.*
51 Barbé-Marbois to Napoleon, May 3, May 23, 1805, *ibid.*
52 Barbé-Marbois to Napoleon, June 7, 1805, *ibid.,* AF[iv] 1087.
53 To Napoleon, May 15, 20, 31, June 3, 21, 1805, *ibid.*
54 *Ibid.*

55 To Napoleon, June 16, 1805, *ibid.*
56 To Napoleon, June 6, 1805, *ibid.*

CHAPTER VIII

1 To Napoleon, August 26, 1805, AN, AF^{iv} 1082.
2 Accounts of the operations of the *Négociants Réunis* are to be found in Louis Adolphe Thiers, *Le Consulat et l'Empire* (Paris 1847), VI, 34–39, 187–99, 375–81; M. Marion, *Histoire financière de la France* (Paris, 1914–28), IV, 275–85; A. Fugier, *Napoléon et l'Espagne* (Paris, 1930), II, 8–22; Georges Lefebvre, *Napoléon* (Paris, 1935), 204–208.
3 To Napoleon, December 27, 1805, AAE, France, Mémoires et Documents, Vol. 1415, fol. 171.
4 Lefebvre, *Napoléon,* 205–206.
5 To Napoleon, February 27, March 13, April 5, 9, 1805, AN, AF^{iv} 1082.
6 To Napoleon, August 20, 21, 1805, *ibid.*
7 The following paragraphs are based primarily on Fugier, *Napoléon et l'Espagne,* II, 17–19.
8 Barbé-Marbois to Napoleon, October 13, 1805, AAE, France, Mémoires et Documents, Vol. 1415, fol. 129; Barbé-Marbois to Napoleon, October 14, 1805, AN, AF^{iv} 1082.
9 Barbé-Marbois to Napoleon, September 28, 1805, *ibid.*
10 Barbé-Marbois to Beurnonville, October 21, 1805, AAE, France, Mémoires et Documents, ff. 130–131^v.
11 AN, AF^{iv} 1082.
12 Barbé-Marbois to Napoleon, October 7, 1805, *ibid.;* Barbé-Marbois to Napoleon, October 11, 1805, AAE, France, Mémoires et Documents, Vol. 1415, fol. 125^v.
13 Barbé-Marbois to Napoleon, November 6, 7, 1805, *ibid.,* ff. 139–39^v.
14 Barbé-Marbois to Napoleon, November 7, 1805, *ibid.,* ff. 141–48.
15 Extract from the report of the minister of police, November 9, 1805, *ibid.,* ff. 202–202^v.

Notes

16 November 9, 1805, *ibid.*, ff. 202ᵛ–203ᵛ.

17 Barbé-Marbois to Napoleon, November 11, 1805, *ibid.*, ff. 149–49ᵛ.

18 Barbé-Marbois to Napoleon, November 12, 1805, *ibid.*, ff. 152–53ᵛ.

19 Barbé-Marbois to Napoleon, November 13, 1805, *ibid.*, ff. 153ᵛ–54.

20 Barbé-Marbois to Napoleon, November 14, 1805, *ibid.*, ff. 155–55ᵛ.

21 Barbé-Marbois to Napoleon, November 19, 1805, *ibid.*, ff. 155ᵛ–56.

22 Barbé-Marbois to Napoleon, November 20, 1805, *ibid.*, ff. 157–58.

23 Barbé-Marbois to Napoleon, November 24, 1805, *ibid.*, ff. 160ᵛ–63.

24 Barbé-Marbois to Napoleon, December 1, 1805, *ibid.*, fol. 163ᵛ.

25 *Correspondance de Napoléon 1ᵉʳ*, XI, 522.

26 Barbé-Marbois to Napoleon, December 7, 1805, AAE, France, Mémoires et Documents, Vol. 1415, ff. 164ᵛ–65ᵛ.

27 Barbé-Marbois to Napoleon, December 16, 1805, *ibid.*, ff. 167–67ᵛ.

28 Barbé-Marbois to Napoleon, December 20, 1805, *ibid.*, ff. 168–69.

29 Barbé-Marbois to Napoleon, December 23, 1805, *ibid.*, ff. 169–70.

30 *Correspondance de Napoléon 1ᵉʳ*, XI, 585.

31 Barbé-Marbois to Napoleon, December 27, 1805, AAE, France, Mémoires et Documents, Vol. 1415, ff. 170ᵛ–71ᵛ.

32 *Ibid.*, fol. 173ᵛ.

33 G. Lacour-Gayet, *Talleyrand, 1754–1838* (Paris, 1928–34), II, 173.

34 Barbé-Marbois to Napoleon, January 7, 1806, AAE, France, Mémoires et Documents, Vol. 1415, ff. 174–74ᵛ.

35 *Correspondance de Napoléon 1ᵉʳ*, XI, 669.

36 Quoted in Fleichmann, *Memoirs of Count Miot de Melito*, 388, footnote.

37 Comte Mollien, *Mémoires d'un Ministre du Trésor Public* (Paris, 1898), I, 432–38.

38 Napoleon to A. M. de Champagny, January 27, 1806, *Correspondance de Napoléon 1er*, XI, 680.

39 To General Berthier, January 27, 1806, *ibid.*, 681.

40 Marion, *Histoire financière de la France*, IV, 285.

41 January 26, 1806, AN, AFiv 1082.

42 F. M. Kircheisen, *Napoleon* (New York, 1932), 343.

43 Note d'Antoine Passy, MSS., Archives de l'Eure.

44 The decree establishing the Cour des Comptes was issued at Fontainebleau, AN, AFiv 272, plaq 1910.

45 Marion, *Histoire financière de la France*, IV, 294–97.

46 *Moniteur,* November 14, 1807; *Centenaire de la Cour des Comptes,* 1807–1907.

47 *Opinions rapports et choix d'écrits politiques de Charles François Lebrun, Duc de Plaisance,* 455–56.

48 Mollien, *Mémoires,* II, 93.

49 Antoine Passy, *Notice sur M. de Barbé-Marbois, lue à la séance publique de la Société Libre d'Agriculture, le 24 septembre 1837* (Évreux, 1838), 25.

50 Marion, *Histoire financière de la France,* IV. 297.

51 Hélot MS.

52 To an unnamed addressee, Paris, July 22, 1811, Archives de l'Eure.

53 Présidence des collèges électoraux, 1812; Procès verbaux du collège électoral de département du département de l'Eure, Archives de l'Eure.

54 *Armorial du Premier Empire* (Paris, 1894), 47.

55 AN, AFiv 753, plaq 6053.

56 J. Mavidal and E. Laurent, *Archives Parlementaires* (Second series; Paris, 1862–68) XI, 662–63.

57 *Ibid.,* 672, Extrait des registres du Sénat Conservateur du mardi 28 décembre 1813, AN, AFiv 841, plaq 6750.

58 Hélot MS.

Notes

CHAPTER IX

1 E. J. Knapton, "Some Aspects of the Bourbon Restoration of 1814," *Journal of Modern History*, VI, (1934), 422.
2 Mavidal and Laurent, *Archives Parlementaires* (Second Series), XII, 8–10.
3 Barbé-Marbois' notes of April 3–6, Hélot MS.
4 *Moniteur,* April 6, 1814.
5 Eugène Forgues (ed.), *Mémoires et relations politiques du Baron de Vitrolles* (Paris, 1884), I, 383–84; Pierre Simon, *L'Élaboration de la charte constitutionnelle de 1814* (Paris, 1906), 38–39.
6 *Ibid.*, 75, 81, 89.
7 Hélot MS.
8 *Moniteur,* May 4, 1814.
9 Barbé-Marbois to commander in chief of the National Guard, Barbé-Marbois to the minister of justice, May 20, 1814, AN, AA5, pièce 310.
10 Mavidal and Laurent, *Archives Parlementaires,* XII, 38.
11 *Ibid.,* XII, 41, 45–46, 51–52, 52–54, 56–57, 89–92.
12 *Ibid.,* XII, 69.
13 *Ibid.,* XII, 667.
14 *Ibid.,* XV, 58; Duvergier de Hauranne, *Histoire du gouvernement parlementaire en France, 1814–48* (Paris, 1857–71), III, 265.
15 Mavidal and Laurent, *Archives Parlementaires,* XIII, 194–97.
16 *Ibid.,* XIII, 492–508.
17 *Ibid.,* XIII, 749–52.
18 Geoffrey Bruun, *Europe and the French Imperium, 1799–1814* (New York, 1938), 197.
19 J. A. Dulaure, *Histoire de la révolution française depuis 1814 jusqu'à 1830* (Paris, 1830–41), IV, 185.
20 *Biographie nouvelle des contemporains* (Paris, n.d.).
21 *Complot d'Arnold et de Sir Henry Clinton contre les États-Unis d'Amérique et contre le général Washington,* septembre

1780, 166. Another edition, with a slightly different title, was published in Paris in 1831.

22 *Ibid.*, vii, x–xi.

23 *Ibid.*, viii.

24 Note of June 27, Hélot MS.

25 "Notes sur l'occupation de la France par les armées étrangères en 1815. Conjectures touchant les vues de l'Autriche sur l'Alsace, la Lorraine, etc." Hélot MS.

26 *Memoirs of the Count of Rochechouart,* 1788–1822 (London, 1920), 285–86.

27 Elizabeth P. Brush, *Guizot in the Early Years of the Orleanist Monarchy* (Urbana, 1929), 22.

28 François Guizot, *Memoirs to Illustrate the History of My Own Times* (London, 1858–61), I, 103–104.

29 S. Charléty, "La Restauration," in Ernest Lavisse, *Histoire de France contemporaine,* IV, (Paris, 1921), 94–96.

30 Charles H. Pouthas, *Guizot pendant la restauration* (Paris, 1923), 117–18.

31 Mavidal and Laurent, *Archives Parlementaires,* XV, 76–7.

32 Duvergier de Hauranne, *Histoire du gouvernement parlementaire en France,* III, 282.

33 Dulaure, *Histoire de la révolution française,* IV, 281.

34 Pouthas, *Guizot pendant la restauration,* 119–20.

35 Duvergier de Hauranne, *Histoire du gouvernement parlementaire en France,* III, 285–86.

36 André Paillet, "Les cours prévôtales," *Revue des deux mondes* (July 1, 1911), 123–49.

37 Mavidal and Laurent, *Archives Parlementaires,* XV, 66–73, 164–65, 167–68, 186–89, 307.

38 Dulaure, *Histoire de la révolution française,* IV, 185–86.

39 Count Ferrand, for instance, was convinced that Barbé-Marbois had arranged in advance for Lavalette's escape—Vicomte de Broc, *Mémoires du Comte Ferrand* (Paris, 1897), 158–59.

40 J. Lucas-Dubreton, *The Restoration and the July Monarchy* (New York, 1929), 24–26.

41 Major John R. Hall, *The Bourbon Restoration* (London, 1909), 168–70.
42 AN, BB^{17a} 1, dossier 44.
43 *Ibid.,* dossier 12.
44 *Ibid.,* dossier 44.
45 When the author visited Vincennes in July, 1937, someone had just placed a vase of fresh flowers on this monument.
46 AN, BB^{17} 1, dossier 15.
47 Pouthas, *Guizot pendant la restauration,* 126; Duvergier de Hauranne, *Histoire du gouvernement parlementaire en France,* III, 290; Louis de Viel-Castel, *Histoire de la restauration* (Paris, 1860–78), IV, 218–19; V, 72–73; Claude Barante, *Souvenirs du Baron de Barante, publiés par son petit-fils Claude Barante* (Paris, 1890–1901), II, 248.
48 Guizot, *Memoirs to Illustrate the History of My Own Times,* I, 135.

CHAPTER X

1 Passy, *Notice sur M. de Barbé-Marbois,* 7.
2 Eulogy by Count Siméon before the Chamber of Peers, January 17, 1838, Mavidal and Laurent, *Archives Parlementaires,* CXV, 60.
3 M. Maffioli, *Essai d'un projet de loi de réorganization de la Cour des Comptes précédé d'une notice historique sur cette institution* (Paris, 1836), 231. The author was "conseiller-référendaire de première classe à la Cour des Comptes."
4 Minister of finance to minister of justice, October 1, 1817; minister of justice to Barbé-Marbois, October 4; Barbé-Marbois to minister of justice, October 5; minister of justice to Marbois, October 9, AN, BB^{17a} 1, dossier 44.
5 Bégin, *Biographie de la Moselle,* 116.
6 They are all listed in the *Catalogue générale des livres imprimés de la Bibliothèque Nationale.*
7 Passy, *Notice sur M. de Barbé-Marbois,* 24.
8 *Ibid.;* Marbois, *Notice sur Barbé-Marbois,* 13–14.

9 Marquis de Marbois, *Précis exact de tout ce qui s'est passé à l'inauguration de la statue de Henri IV. Discours prononcé à Sa Majesté. Inauguration de la statue de Henri IV, du 25 août 1818* (Paris, 1818), 4 pages. Bibliothèque Nationale.

10 *Visite des prisons des départements de l'Eure et de la Seine Inférieure. Par un membre de la Société Royale pour l'amélioration des prisons* (Paris, 1819), 44. Bibliothèque Nationale. *Rapport sur l'état actuel des prisons dans les départements du Calvados, de l'Eure, de la Manche, et de la Seine-Inférieure; et sur la maison de correction de Gaillon.* October, 1823. À son Altesse Royale Mgr. le duc d'Angoulême (Paris, 1824). Bibliothèque Nationale.

11 P. M. S. Catineau-Laroche, *De la Guyane française, de son état physique, de son agriculture, de son régime intérieur et du projet de la peupler avec les laboureurs Européens: ou examen d'un écrit de M. le Marquis de Barbé-Marbois sur le même sujet* (Paris, 1822). The author is much annoyed at Marbois' opposition and indulges in a number of personal remarks at his expense.

12 Barbé-Marbois, *Journal d'un déporté*, I, iii–iv.

13 *Observations sur les votes de quarante-un conseils généraux de département concernant la déportation des forçats libérés présentées à Monsieur Le Dauphin par un membre de la Société Royale pour l'amélioration des prisons* (Paris, 1828). Bibliothèque Nationale.

14 *Moniteur,* January 3, 1825.

15 Marbois to Monroe, June 6, 1821, Monroe Papers, New York Public Library.

16 Marbois to Monroe, June 6, 1821 (second letter of this date), *ibid.* He thanks Monroe for recommending some Americans to him. His daughter and son-in-law join in thanking Monroe for the opportunity of welcoming the President's friends.

17 August 18, 1822, *ibid.* This, and all the other letters here cited from the Monroe Papers, are printed in the author's "Barbé-Marbois and His *Histoire de la Louisiane.*"

18 Monroe Papers, New York Public Library.

19 James Brown to James Monroe, Paris, April 15, 1824, James A. Padgett (ed.), "Some Letters of James Brown of Louisiana to Presidents of the United States," *Louisiana Historical Quarterly,* XX, (1937), 98.

20 To Monroe, May 22, 1824, Monroe Papers, New York Public Library.

21 Brown to Monroe, January 20, 1825, Padgett, "Some Letters of James Brown," 121.

22 To Marbois, March 25, 1827, Monroe Papers, New York Public Library.

23 To Monroe, June 28, 1827, Padgett, "Some Letters of James Brown," 129.

24 To Monroe, June 6, 1827, Monroe Papers, New York Public Library.

25 Count de la Ferronnays, minister of foreign affairs, to Marbois, July 15, 1828; Sparks to Marbois, Hôtel de Windsor, Rue de Rivoli, July 16; Marbois to Sparks, July 17, Sparks MSS, Harvard College Library.

26 Marbois to Sparks, July 23, 1828; de Lanay, minister of war, to Marbois, August 21; Marbois to Sparks, August 24, *ibid.*

27 Sparks to Marbois, July 21, August 5, 1828; Marbois to Sparks, August 5, 13, *ibid.*

28 Sparks to Marbois, August 27, 1828, *ibid.* Sparks had the translation done in Paris by a Mr. Lawrence, recent American chargé d'affaires in London—Herbert B. Adams, *Life and Writings of Jared Sparks* (Boston and New York, 1893), II, 118.

29 *Histoire de la Louisiane et de la cession de cette colonie par la France aux États-Unis de l'Amérique Septentrionale; précédée d'un discours sur la Constitution et le gouvernement des États-Unis* (Paris, 1829), 485; *The History of Louisiana, Particularly of the Cession of That Colony to the United States of America; with an Introductory Essay on the Constitution and Government of the United States.* By Barbé-Marbois. Translated from the French by an American citizen (Philadelphia, 1830).

30 This and the two following paragraphs are reproduced with some changes from the author's article, "Barbé-Marbois and His *Histoire de la Louisiane*," 358–60.

31 See Lyon, *Louisiana in French Diplomacy,* 191–207, for a more extended discussion of the motives that led Napoleon to sell Louisiana.

32 XXVIII (1829), 389–418. The American edition was briefly reviewed on its appearance the following year, XXX (1830), 551–56.

33 To Monroe, April 3, 1829, Monroe Papers, New York Public Library.

34 To Marbois, June 24, 1829, Monroe Papers, Library of Congress.

35 Monroe corresponded with a number of people about the book. He sent a copy to Fulwar Skipwith, of Louisiana, who had been in Paris in 1803, and Skipwith replied on June 8, 1829, supporting some of Monroe's statements (Monroe Papers, New York Public Library). Monroe criticized the book in a letter of May 2, 1829, to Lafayette—S. M. Hamilton (ed.), *The Writings of James Monroe* (New York, 1903), VII, 202–204. He also mentioned the volume to Joseph Bonaparte on December 21, 1829 (*ibid.,* VII, 206).

36 Marbois to Sparks, July 23, 1828; Sparks to Marbois, July 24, Sparks MSS., Harvard College Library.

37 *North American Review,* XXVIII (1829), 389.

38 Bégin, *Biographie de la Moselle,* 135.

39 *Moniteur,* July 19, August 7, 21, 1830, and January 2, 1831.

40 Lettre du Baron Atthalin priant le Marquis de Marbois de servir du témoin au marriage de la princesse Louise avec le roi des Belges 1832. Catalogue of Saffroy frères, 1910.

41 *Nouvelle biographie générale* (Paris, 1852–77).

42 *Biographie des hommes du jour* (Paris, 1835), 127.

43 Marbois, *Notice sur Barbé-Marbois,* 14.

44 Extract from the *Moniteur,* April 7, 1834, preserved at the *Cour des Comptes* in the *Collection des lois, sénatus-consultes, décrets, ordonnances et autres documents concernant la Cour des*

Comptes, 1807–1880. Formée sous la direction de M. Dufresne.

45 Lucas Dubreton, *The Restoration and the July Monarchy*, 233–37.

46 *Biographie des hommes du jour,* 122, 127.

47 Donation par M. Pierre François Barbé, Marquis de Marbois, premier président de la Cour des Comptes, pair de France, grand cordon de l'ordre royale de la Légion d'Honneur, demt ordinairement à Paris, hôtel de la Cour des Comptes, étant alors en son château de Noyers, canton de Gisors, à la commune de Noyers, ce accepté, par M. J. B. Roycourt Maire, Archives de l'Eure, Évreux.

48 Passy, *Notice sur M. de Marbois,* 28–31; Mavidal and Laurent, *Archives Parlementaires,* CXV, 60.

49 Passy, *Notice sur M. de Marbois,* 28.

50 Archives de l'Eure, Évreux.

51 L'inventaire après le décès, arrivé à Paris le 12 janvier 1837, de M. François Barbé, Marquis de Marbois (copy), Archives de l'Eure, Évreux.

52 Around 1841 she began an affair with the Prince of Belgiojoso and lived with him on Lake Como from 1843 to 1853. She returned to Greece in 1853 and died near Athens on May 14, 1854. Lebrun lived to become a senator of the Second Empire, dying in Paris on January 21, 1859. Jean Julien Barbé, *À travers le vieux Metz: les maisons historiques* (Metz, 1937), 97–99. Notes, Archives de l'Eure, Évreux.

53 *Journal des Débats,* January 14, 17, 1837; *Moniteur,* January 17, 1837; *La Charte de 1830*, Paris, January 18, 1837.

54 To M. Villemain, Noyers, October 8, 1832, Archives de l'Eure, Évreux.

Index

233